The Books of
KAHLIL GIBRAN

The Madman · 1918

Twenty Drawings · 1919

The Forerunner · 1920

The Prophet · 1923

Sand and Foam · 1926

Jesus the Son of Man · 1928

The Earth Gods · 1931

The Wanderer · 1932

The Garden of the Prophet · 1933

Prose Poems · 1934

Nymphs of the Valley · 1948

Spirits Rebellious · 1948

A Tear and a Smile · 1950

. .

Beloved Prophet:
The Love Letters of Kahlil Gibran
and Mary Haskell
Edited by Virginia Hilu

This Man from Lebanon:
A Study of Kahlil Gibran
by Barbara Young

PUBLISHED BY ALFRED A. KNOPF

A TEAR

AND A SMILE

A TEAR
AND A SMILE

BY

KAHLIL GIBRAN

Translated from the Arabic by

H. M. NAHMAD

With an Introduction by

ROBERT HILLYER

1976

NEW YORK : ALFRED·A·KNOPF

Published February 20, 1960
Reprinted twenty-one times
Twenty-third printing, October 1976

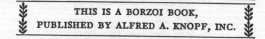

THIS IS A BORZOI BOOK,
PUBLISHED BY ALFRED A. KNOPF, INC.

Manufactured in the United States of America and distributed by Random House, Inc. Published in Canada by Random House of Canada, Limited

TO

M·E·H

I offer this book, the first breath in the tem-
pest of my life, to that noble spirit who loves
with the breeze and walks with the tempests.

GIBRAN

✳

TO YVONNE

FROM THE TRANSLATOR

INTRODUCTION
by Robert Hillyer

A Tear and a Smile includes much of Kahlil
Gibran's earliest work, and, with the interesting
prose poem written in Paris on his twenty-fifth
birthday, marks the beginning of a more mature
and affirmative response to life. Like those of many
romantic poets, of the East or the West, his youthful flights were toward the white radiance of eternity, away from a world that seemed largely in the
hands of injustice and violence. The recoil of a sen-
sitive mind from reality frequently takes revolu-
tionary forms of which political revolution is merely
the most obvious. With Gibran the revolt was not
directed toward institutions so much as toward the
individuals who became the accomplices of abstract
evil, of greed, injustice, and bloodshed. Most of the
human figures in his early works are therefore per-
sonifications, with the result that parable and alle-
gory are the usual method. His later works, more
frankly homiletic, gain from the abandonment of
the indirect narrative style and present a bolder ac-
ceptance of hope for felicity in the here and now.

It is not to be wondered at that in all his works,

of whatever period, the teeming memories of his ancient homeland suggest his landscape and metaphors as well as the cast of his thought. Syria and the Near East, though so much smaller geographically than the Far East, present a richer profusion of contrasting lights and shadows, where, in Bridges' superlative couplet,

> . . . in her Mediterranean mirror gazing Old Asia's dreamy face wrinkleth to a westward smile.

In the Far East two gigantic civilizations have stood guard for thousands of years in monolithic grandeur, intricate in detail but almost unbroken in contour. The Near East, in contrast, has been built up, leveled, built up again in strata of cultures reaching back to the dawn of man. Furthermore, it has been a sounding-board against which Europe speaks and whence the echoes return magnified. The prehistoric Greeks, crossing the Hellespont, founded Troy between the peaks of Ida and Samothrace, and from there the clash of arms vibrated back across the Homeric lyre. From the Eastern Empire, centuries later, Byzantium provided the first patterns for Italian medieval art. And nowhere except in India has mysticism sown more fertile fields, where religion blossomed with appropriate luxuriance in an earthly soil so thin.

Lebanon, the native country of Kahlil Gibran, has its full share of such associations. The rites of the ancient church of Antioch are performed within a stone's throw of a ruined temple. The young girls of Christian faith cast flowers into the spring freshets that course down from Mount Lebanon, unaware that they are celebrating the return of Adonis from the realms of death. In "Before the Throne of Beauty" Gibran pictures Nature as a young girl who is the daughter of the forests. She says to him: "I am the virgin whom your forefathers did adore; for whom they builded altars and shrines and temples in Baalbek and Aphaca and Byblos." The poet answers: "Those temples are destroyed and the bones of my forefathers lie level with the earth and naught remains of their gods and their ways save a few pages between the covers of books." "Many of the gods," she tells him, "live in the life of their adorers and die in their death. Others of them live eternally and forever." Thus to the young Syrian poet the search for what lives on when the stones fall and the statues crumble led him often to contemplation among the ruins of a civilization that had collapsed into the debris of others preceding it: the marts, the churches, the fortresses, the Roman temples.

In the portico of such a temple young Gibran observed on his early morning walks a solitary man sitting on the drum of a fallen column and staring into the east. At last he grew bold enough to address the man and ask him what he was doing.

"I am looking at life," was the answer.

"Oh, is that all?"

"Isn't that enough?"

The incident made an impression on Gibran. Somewhere in one of his books he has set it down. I tell it as I remember it from his lips.

The observer of life seated amid the ruins of the

past, yet looking toward the coming day; who is alone, unencumbered by the clamor of the city and the collision with other minds: this watcher for the dawn would seem to be Gibran's conception of the poet. "The moon drew a fine veil across the City of the Sun and stillness enveloped all creation. And the awesome ruins rose like giants mocking at nocturnal things. In that hour two forms without substance appeared out of the void like mist ascending from the surface of a lake. They sat them on a marble column which time had wrenched from that wondrous edifice, and looked down upon a scene that spoke of enchanted places. . . . 'These are the remains of those shrines that I builded for you, my beloved; and there the ruins of a palace I raised for your pleasure. . . . No thing remains save the particles of love created by your beauty and the beauty your love brought to life.' " But beyond the ruins and even the memories of mortal love there is "the divinity of man standing upright as a giant mocking at earth's foolishness and the anger of the elements. And like a pillar of light standing out of the ruins of Babylon and Nineveh and Palmyra, and Bombay and San Francisco, it sang a hymn of immortality saying: 'Let the earth then take what is to it; for I am without end.' "

Gibran's figure of the Poet stands at the top of his hierarchy, far and away the highest of mankind. As contemplation of the stars may lift the spirit of some, or the sea the spirit of others, so in Gibran's case the background of his time-scarred country provided a vision of the great and the small, the many and the one, the things that perish and the things that endure, which is the measuring-rod of the poets. Damascus and Lebanon were his earliest memories and from that landscape, similar to the one we imagine in reading the Old Testament, he drew his references. He became an exile; he lived for a time in Paris and finally settled in New York, where he was known to many during the first three decades of the century, but he never let go the sinewy hand of his parent country. The unhurried courtesy of the East was in his gestures, her silences and sounds were still with him, and at times he spoke with homesick awe of the customs of the church of Syria, against whose orthodoxy he had long since rebelled.

In his youthful revolt against priestcraft he showed a spiritual affinity to the English poet William Blake. As time went on, other aspects of the Occidental mystic's philosophy combined to influence Gibran's writings and his drawings as well. The kinship was clearly discernible and acknowledged. Many convictions were common to both: a hatred of sham and binding orthodoxy, personified by evil priests; the manumission of physical love from the bonds of convention in order to attain spiritual completeness; the perception of beauty in the moment that seems to be fleeting but is, in truth, everlasting; and the discovery of miracles in seasonal nature and the commonplace things of daily living. Both warred against reason in the name of imagination. Both defied the snares of logic to cut a straight wingpath directly to God.

To both Blake and Gibran these revelations are the gift of the poet. The Poet and the Prophet are one. The familiar and majestic lines of Blake express the bardic ideal:

> Hear the voice of the Bard,
> Who present, past, and future, sees;
> Whose ears have heard
> The Holy Word
> That walk'd among the ancient trees. . . .

And in the present volume we read these lines from "A Poet's Voice":

> Say of me what you will and the morrow will judge you, and your words shall be a witness before its judging and a testimony before its justice. . . . I came to say a word and I shall utter it. Should death take me ere I give voice, the morrow shall utter it. . . . That which alone I do today shall be proclaimed before the people in days to come.

In Gibran's *Prophet* a separate character is assigned to the Poet, yet they are two aspects of the same entity, the highest emanation of Man. The poet can sin only in denying his own nature — and in all Gibran's pages no poet commits such a sin. Even in conversation with friends Gibran maintained the same high seriousness toward what was to him a sacred office. I remember one afternoon over thirty years ago in Gibran's studio. Young and easily embarrassed, I had let fall an evasive and perhaps frivolous remark in response to a characterization of me as a young poet. It was trifling; I have forgotten it. But I have not forgotten how

Gibran looked at me long and intently as if searching out my real nature, and at last made some observation on the sacredness of poetry and the high calling of its votaries, which disposed of any possibility of touching the subject lightly. "Ah," he concluded, "but you must not talk that way, you must not do the usual things that other men do, for a poet is holy." A lifetime passion was behind the quiet rebuke.

"The Poet's Death Is His Life" is a dialogue between the poet and Death, showing Death as the poet's friend and consummate love, who alone can set his spirit free and, as men are gradually enlightened, endow with his prophecies a fairer world. We approach here a conception of the poet as one who gives his life for the redemption of mankind. The logical assumption that Jesus was the ultimate Poet was to Gibran a not unnatural conclusion.

More orthodox conceptions of Christ, as formulated by the churches, were repulsive to him. If the Poet was incapable of wrong, the Priest, at least in these early works, could do no right. Again we are reminded of Blake:

And priests in black gowns were walking their
    rounds,
And binding with briers my joys and desires.

In *Nymphs of the Valley* we read the story of the poor boy tormented by the wicked monks; in *Spirits Rebellious* it is the Priest who pronounces the curse over the bodies of the bride and her lover who died faithful to their love.

We of the West cannot weigh the factual truth of

xiii

Gibran's portrayal of the priesthood in his youthful works. It may be that the Syrian Church of his boyhood was indeed the purveyor of corruption, the jeweled bauble empty of significance, the oppressor of the poor, as he describes it. Remnants of Byzantine splendor along with Byzantine decay may cling to the Eastern churches; the poet's indignation cannot be wholly without reference to observed conditions. The Eastern churches have never undergone the purgation by heresy and reformation that has cleansed the Western churches.

Yet it must be remembered that the Oriental method of personifying institutions and summoning an entire situation into one symbol was characteristic of Gibran's work, especially in his novitiate as poet. Truth to a large design, as in Byzantine art, sometimes demanded the distortion of details. His realism consisted in the massing of general effects to emphasize concepts that he believed to be the ultimate reality. Thus he was at the opposite pole from contemporary realists who overwhelm large themes in an avalanche of careful detail. In this fact lies much of Gibran's appeal for the reader who wearies of the modern Occidental technique, which so often leads to the gutter and away from the stars. The photographic reproduction of actuality with no reference to the more expansive designs of Truth and Justice, Beauty and Peace, would have held no interest for Gibran.

In this symbolic usage, parallel to the good Poet and the bad Priest, we find the Poor Man, who is always oppressed, and the Rich Man, who is always the oppressor. In infancy the Prince's son is hailed with songs of praise as one who "will be to you a pride and delight and the heir to the inheritance of my great forefathers. Rejoice then . . . for your future now belongs to this scion of our house." At the same time a poverty-stricken woman gives birth to her son, and "when the noise of the multitudes in the streets had died the wretched woman placed the infant in her lap and looked into its shining eyes, and she wept as though she would baptize the child with her tears. 'Have compassion on us, O Lord!' " And thus the separate destinies of the rich and the poor are spun out until even in death the division persists, as in "The City of the Dead":

The funeral of a rich and powerful one. The remains of the dead followed by the quick, who wept and wailed and filled the ether with crying and lament.

The procession reached the burial ground. The priests prayed . . . and the musicians blew upon their trumpets. Others spoke and praised the departed with fine words. . . .

The sun inclined toward the west, and the shadow of rocks and trees lengthened and Nature began to shed her garments of light.

On that very moment I looked and beheld two men bearing a wooden casket. Behind them came a woman in rags carrying a suckling child. By her side trotted a dog, looking now at her, now at the casket. It was the funeral procession of a poor man, a humble man. . . .

And I looked toward the City of the Living,

saying within myself: "That belongs to the wealthy and the mighty." And toward the City of the Dead I said: "This too belongs to the wealthy and the mighty. Where then, O Lord, is the home of the poor and the weak?"

Having thus spoken, I lifted my eyes to the clouds, whose edges were colored with gold by the rays of the setting sun. And a voice within me said: "Yonder."

In spite of the impressiveness of the conclusion, we are aware that the symbolic method in such a story is far too generalized to support the scrutiny of truth. It becomes little more than sentimentalism, gilded by the rays of uncertain artistry. Sentimentalism of this kind is the prevailing weakness of young romantics, including, at times, the young Blake.

With the Poor Man and the Priest, the Lover completes the trinity of noble personages. In the early parables physical union, but delicately hinted at, is the consummation, the release of the soul. There is no sustained emphasis on the sensualism we associate with the love poetry of the Orient, and even the discernible echoes from the *Song of Songs* are chastened and become rather remote. In "The Tale of a Friend" we are told that "love comes in many guises. Sometimes it is as wisdom, other times justice, ofttimes hope. My love for him was my hope that the strong light of its sun might triumph over the darkness of transient sorrows. But I knew not when and where filthiness became a clean thing, and cruelty kindness, and ignorance wisdom. A man knows not in what manner the spirit is freed from matter until after it is freed."

Death is the ultimate lover. It may come as a king whose hand is laid upon the lost shepherd; it may come as a woman of unearthly beauty clothed in a garment white as snow. It is life itself in perfected form. "Life and death are one, even as the river and the sea are one. . . . How shall you find it unless you seek it in the heart of life?" Again, "Only when you drink from the river of silence shall you indeed sing." Death is that goal toward which we yearn, whether or not we know it, in the depth of our being. The identification of death as the climax of all human passion is no less akin to the concluding theories of Sigmund Freud than to the love-death of Tristan and Isolde.

The life after death, however, is a separate theme that undergoes a change through Gibran's writings. The early stories indicate a belief in the doctrine of reincarnation that seems more than a literary device. In *Nymphs of the Valley* there is the story of the lovers who meet again after two thousand years in the ruins of the temple of Astarte, and there complete the noble passion that was frustrated so long before, by the priests of a faith whose altars now lie open to the wind and rain. But later Gibran seems to have joined the neo-Platonists in their belief in the return of the individual soul to God.

Evidently Gibran left behind him very early his childhood conception of individual redemption and survival as taught in Christianity. In the theory of reincarnation of the soul the identity half persists through a succession of new experiences with no recollection of what has gone before except in occasional flashes of revelation. At last he surrendered his last vestige of belief in the survival of the individual and spoke of the reunion of that particle of deity, that small kingdom of God within each man, with the all-embracing Godhead. The rest is the dross of this world, gratefully to be relinquished as the soul takes its lonely flight back to its Source.

A Tear and a Smile exhibits this somewhat emotional philosophy at its most untamed. If the parables and observations lack the serenity of *The Prophet* or *The Madman,* they have some compensating vigor, almost a rashness, of approach, natural to a young writer who, had he been born in the West, would have been a late recruit to the romantic school. The book is more Eastern, however, than his later writings. It is probable that in these Arabic compositions he was writing for his countrymen at home and in exile. That is a larger audience than many are aware of, and international in scope.

In the beginning of this volume we are told that the tear of sorrow purifies the heart and that the smile of joy warms it with understanding. Spiritual hunger is the goal of life; the quest is its own fulfillment. To realize a dream is to lose it, and the satisfied of this world are the most wretched of people. Divested of personification, these ideas may be presented without sentimentalism. They are best left undramatized, and that fact was borne in upon the maturing poet. There are, however, certain figures already known to history or literature who lend themselves as symbols, and when they are available, the union of drama and philosophy becomes inevitable. This method Gibran seldom used. He avoided personal names freighted with meaning. It is interesting to note, however, that the great Danish poet Johannes V. Jensen used Christopher Columbus as the embodiment of exactly the same idea of spiritual hunger being the goal of life so frequently found in Gibran's parables. Toward the end of Jensen's poem "Christopher Columbus," Columbus comes to understand that the realization of a dream destroys it:

For when he discovers the saving isle, his visions
    flee;
A new world is wedged between his soul and the
    ultimate sea.

The contrast in expression between the Northern and the Eastern mysticism is worth mentioning.

Gibran's strength developed not from a change of technique but from a change in emphasis. It would be unnatural for a mature poet to continue to express nothing but loathing for the world in which he lives, and always to point "yonder." Such grimly maintained irony in English and American poetry of the past generation has resulted in a wasteland of lamentations which, on analysis, prove to be but the vulgar exposure of personal woes and inadequacies. The phrasing is tough, but the core is effeminate. Poetry cannot proceed along a series of negations. Gibran's best work, embellished though it is with Asian metaphor, develops manlier qualities. Hope, cheerfulness, and anger displace the perhaps overworked tears and smiles, and they increase as the poet grows older.

The second half of the present volume is in the main given over to these more positive moods. "The Widow and Her Son" is a dignified little *genre* piece wherein the treasure of the humble is adequately realized. Patriotism is the inspiration of "A People and Destiny," wherein Syria, personified as a shepherdess, consults with Destiny, in the guise of an old man, with something keener than mere wistfulness for a vanished past. "Behold the sun rising from out of darkness" — the conclusion of "Peace" — becomes gradually the prevailing theme. The Sun, moreover, is not only that eventual and spiritual orb to be reached through the gates of suffering and death, but the good daily sun, warming the earth to a genial response, a felicity in the here and now, an assurance of terrestrial bliss.

Thus in his first flights the poet sped toward eternity and saw the world as a place where misfortune must purify the soul for its reunion with God. Then the increasing warmth of life led him to be less dualistic: the material world became informed with the heavenly light. Gibran's ripened philosophy is anticipated in several of the selections here, prominently in "My Birthday," written in Paris when he became twenty-five. In this piece he explicitly turns away from his past writings and drawings in the sudden arrival of a joy he had not imagined: a meaning in the faces of people, their voices rising upward in the streets of the city, children at play, young men and old, and so beyond that city, not in escape but in understanding, to "the wild parts in their awful beauty and voiced silence," then on to the sea, the stars, and "all the contending . . .

forces of attraction and repulsion . . . created and borne by that Will, timeless and without limit." We are reminded of the climax of Victor Hugo's famous "Extase":

Et les étoiles d'or, légions infinies,
A voix haute, à voix basse, avec mille harmonies,
Disaient, en inclinant leurs couronnes de feu;
Et les flots bleus, que rien ne gouverne et n'arrête,
Disaient, en recourbant l'écume de leur crête:
— C'est le Seigneur, le Seigneur Dieu!

At the end Gibran discovers and acknowledges that "humanity is the spirit of divineness on earth," and "what I now say with one tongue, tomorrow will say with many."

The poet grows up. The detestable Priests and Rich Men disappear; the impeccable Poets and Lovers take on more lively attributes than mere flawlessness. Eternity becomes more than a distant star wherein we shall quench the small, wandering fire of our being. It begins to shine through the earth, not away from it.

Beauty itself must take on earthly form if it is to summon humanity toward its own perfection. As Gibran says in one of the finest pieces in this book, "The Child Jesus": "My life was a tale of woe; now it is become a joyful thing. And it will be turned to bliss, for the arms of the Child have enfolded my heart and embraced my soul."

CONTENTS

A TEAR

AND A SMILE

THE FOUR ILLUSTRATIONS

IN THIS VOLUME

ARE REPRODUCED FROM

ORIGINAL DRAWINGS BY

THE AUTHOR

A TEAR AND A SMILE

I would not exchange the sorrows of my heart for the joys of the multitude. And I would not have the tears that sadness makes to flow from my every part turn into laughter. I would that my life remain a tear and a smile.

A tear to purify my heart and give me understanding of life's secrets and hidden things. A smile to draw me nigh to the sons of my kind and to be a symbol of my glorification of the gods.

A tear to unite me with those of broken heart; a smile to be a sign of my joy in existence.

I would rather that I died in yearning and longing than that I lived weary and despairing.

I want the hunger for love and beauty to be in the depths of my spirit, for I have seen those who are satisfied the most wretched of people. I have heard the sigh of those in yearning and longing, and it is sweeter than the sweetest melody.

With evening's coming the flower folds her petals

and sleeps, embracing her longing. At morning's approach she opens her lips to meet the sun's kiss.

The life of a flower is longing and fulfillment. A tear and a smile.

The waters of the sea become vapor and rise and come together and are a cloud.

And the cloud floats above the hills and valleys until it meets the gentle breeze, then falls weeping to the fields and joins with the brooks and rivers to return to the sea, its home.

The life of clouds is a parting and a meeting. A tear and a smile.

And so does the spirit become separated from the greater spirit to move in the world of matter and pass as a cloud over the mountain of sorrow and the plains of joy to meet the breeze of death and return whence it came.

To the ocean of Love and Beauty — to God.

THE LIFE OF LOVE

SPRING

Come, my beloved, let us walk among the little hills, for the snows have melted and life is awakened from its sleep and wanders through the hills and valleys.

Come, let us follow the footsteps of spring in the far-off field;

Come and we will ascend the heights and look upon the waving greenness of the plains below.

The dawn of spring has unfolded the garment concealed by the winter night, and the peach tree and the apple wear it, adorned as brides on the Night of Power.

The vines are awakened, their tendrils entwined like the embrace of lovers.

The streams run and leap among the rocks singing songs of rejoicing.

The flowers are bursting forth from the heart of Nature as foam from the crest of sea waves.

Come, my beloved, let me drink of the last of rain's tears from narcissus cups and make full our spirits of the joyful songs of birds.

Let us breathe the scent of the breeze and sit by yonder rock where hides the violet, and give and take of Love's kisses.

SUMMER

Arise, my love, to the field, for the days of the harvest are come and the time of reaping is nigh.

The grain is ripened by the sun in the warmth of its love to Nature;

Come ere the birds reap the fruits of our labor, and the ants consume our land.

Come, let us garner the earth's yield as the spirit does grains of bliss from fulfillment's sowing in the depths of our hearts,

And fill our bins with Nature's bounty as Life does the storehouses of our souls.

Come, my mate, let us make the grass our couch and the heavens our coverlet.

Lay us down our heads on a pillow of soft hay and seek thereon repose from the toil of the day and hearken to the music of the murmur of the brook in the valley.

AUTUMN

Let us go to the vineyard, my love, and press the grapes and store the wine thereof in vessels as the spirit stores the wisdom of ages.

Let us gather the fruits and distill from the flowers their fragrance.

Let us return to the dwellings, for the leaves of the trees are become yellow and the winds have scattered them to make of them a burial shroud for flowers that died grieving at summer's passing.

Come, for the birds have taken flight to the seashore bearing upon their wings the good cheer of the gardens, bequeathing desolation to the jasmine and the myrtle, and the last tears have been shed upon the sod.

Come, let us go, for the brooks have ceased their flowing and the springs are no more, for the tears of their joy are dried up; and the hillocks have cast aside their fine garments.

Come, beloved. For Nature is overcome by sleep and bids farewell to wakefulness with sad and wishful melody.

WINTER

Draw nigh unto me, my soul-mate. Draw nigh and let not icy breath separate our bodies. Sit you with me by this fireside, for fire is winter's fruit.

Speak with me of things of the ages, for mine ears are wearied of the winds' sighing and the elements' lamenting.

Make fast door and window, for the angry face of Nature makes sad my spirit, and to look upon the city beneath the snows, sitting like a mother bereaved, causes my heart to bleed.

Fill you, then, the lamp with oil, for it is already dim. Put it beside you that I may see what the nights have writ on your face. Bring hither the wine-jar that we may drink and remember the days of the pressing.

Draw nigh to me, loved of my spirit, for the fire is dying and ashes conceal it.

Embrace me, for the lamp is dimmed and darkness has conquered it.

Heavy are our eyes with the wine of years.

Look on me with your sleep-darkened eyes. Embrace me ere slumber embrace us. Kiss me, for the snows have prevailed over all save your kiss.

Ah, my beloved one, how deep is the ocean of sleep! How distant the morning . . . in this night!

A TALE

On the banks of that river in the shade of the walnut and the willow sat a farmer's son, gazing quietly at the running water. A youth, he was reared among the meadows where everything spoke of love. Where the branches embraced and the flowers inclined one to another and the birds dallied. Where nature in its all preached the gospel of the Spirit.

A youth of twenty years he was, and yestereve he had seen sitting by the spring a maiden among other maidens and he loved her. But he heard tell that she was the daughter of a Prince and he blamed his heart and complained in his self. Yet blaming does not draw away the heart from love, neither does reproof drive away the spirit from the truth. For a man stands between his heart and his soul as a tender branch in the path of the south wind and the north wind.

The youth looked and saw the violet growing by the side of the daisy, and he heard the nightingale

9

calling out to the blackbird, and he wept in his aloneness and his solitude. And so passed the hours of his love before his eyes like the passing of phantom forms. Then he spoke, his affection overflowing with his words and tears, and said:

"Thus does love mock and make jest of me and lead me whither hope is reckoned an error and longing a despised thing. Love, which I have adored, has lifted my heart to a Prince's palace and brought low my state to a peasant's hut and led my spirit to the beauty of a nymph of paradise guarded by men and protected by honor. . . .

"I am obedient, O Love. What then do you desire? I did follow you along fiery paths, and the flames consumed me. I did open mine eyes and saw naught save darkness; and loosed my tongue, but spoke not save in grief. Yearning embraced me, O Love, with a hunger of the spirit that will not cease except with the kiss of the beloved. I am enfeebled, O Love. Whyfor do you contend with me, you that are strong?

"Whyfor do you oppress me, you that are just? Whyfor do you abandon me, you that are my existence?

"If my blood flows not save by your willing, then pour it out. If my feet move save upon your path, then shrivel them. Do your will in this body, but let my soul rejoice in these meadows, safe in the shadow of your wings. . . .

10

"The stream goes to the sea, its lover, and the flower smiles at its impassioned, the light, and the cloud descends to its valley, its desired. But there is in me what the brook does not know nor the flower hear nor the cloud understand. Behold me alone in my love, separate in my passion, far off from her who wants me not, a soldier in her father's armies or a servant in her palace."

And the youth became silent for a while as though he would learn speech from the murmur of the river and the rustle of leaves on the boughs. Then he said:

"O you whose name I fear to pronounce, O one concealed from me behind coverings of might and walls of majesty, O being of another world whose meeting I dare not covet save in eternity, where all stand equal, O one to whom the strong show obeisance, before whom heads are bowed, to whom treasure-houses are opened:

"You have possessed a heart sanctified by love, and enslaved a soul ennobled by God, and captivated a mind that was yesterday free with the freedom of the fields. Today it has become a captive of passion.

"I have looked on you, O fair creature, and know now the reason of my coming into this world. And when I knew of your lofty state and saw my humbleness, I learned that the gods possess secrets unknown to men and ways wherein they lead spirits where love holds rule without the laws of mankind. When I looked into your eyes it was told me beyond all doubting that this life is but a paradise whose door is the human heart.

"I saw your grandeur and my lowliness locked in struggle and knew that this earth was no more a resting-place for me. When I did find you sitting among your women, as the rose among the myrtle plants, I bethought me that the bride of my dreams had taken body and was become flesh like myself. But on my knowing your father's glory I perceived beyond the rose thorns to prick the fingers. What dreams had united, awakening parted. . . ."

The youth rose to his feet and walked toward the spring, cast down in spirit and broken in heart. And in him despair and grief spoke these words:

"Come, O Death, and deliver me, for the earth, whose thorns do strangle its flowers, is no longer a habitable place. Arise now and save me from days that would wrest love from its seat of glory and put in its stead worldly might. Deliver me, O Death! For eternity is more sweet than the world for a trysting-place of lovers. Yonder shall I await my beloved; there shall I be joined with her."

He came to the spring, and evening was nigh and the sun was lifting her golden mantle from off the meadow. There he sat and wept tears that fell to the ground on which the feet of the Princess had trod.

12

His head fell forward on his breast as though to prevent his heart's flight.

Upon that minute from beyond the willow trees a maiden appeared, dragging the ends of her garment on the grass. She stopped by the youth and put her soft hand on his head. He looked up at her like a sleeper awaked by the sun's rays. He saw standing before him the daughter of the Prince, upon which he fell on his knees and prostrated himself as did Moses before the burning bush. He wished to speak, but no words came, so his tearfilled eyes took the place of his tongue. Then the girl embraced him and kissed his lips and his eyes, sucking in their hot tears, and said in a voice of flute-like clearness:

"I have seen you, my love, in my dreaming and looked upon your face in my aloneness. You are my spirit's companion whom I did lose, and my beautiful half that was separated from it on my coming into this world. I have come in secret, my darling, to meet with you, and now do I behold you in my arms. Have not fear, for I have forsaken my father's glory to follow you to the very ends of the world and drink with you the cup of Life and Death.

"Arise my love and let us go to distant places away from mankind."

There on the outskirts of the land the scouts of the Prince happened upon two human skeletons. On

13

the neck of one was a necklet of gold, and near them both was a stone upon which were written these words:

"Love has joined us; then who shall put us asunder? Death has taken us; and who shall bring us back?"

IN THE CITY OF THE DEAD

I freed myself yesterday from the clamor of the city and walked in the quiet fields until I gained the heights, which Nature had clothed in her choicest garments.

There I stood and beheld the city below, with its high buildings and fine mansions standing beneath dense clouds of smoke rising from factories. I sat myself down observing from afar the works of man and found them a trouble and a stress. I tried in my heart to forget what men had wrought and I turned my eyes toward the field, the throne of God's glory, and beheld in its midst a burial ground. Monuments of stone surrounded by cypress trees.

And so did I sit between the City of the Living and the City of the Dead. Yonder I sat thinking on the never ending strife and ceaseless movement in the one and the quiet that reigned over and the peace that dwelled in the other. Here, hope and despair and love and hate; poverty and riches, belief

15

and unbelief. There, earth within earth that Nature turned over and in the stillness of night created therefrom first plant, then animal life.

Whilst I thus gave myself to these reflections my eyes were drawn to a knot of people walking along preceded by music whose sad refrains filled the air. A procession of pomp and circumstance wherein marched all manner of persons. The funeral of a rich and powerful one. The remains of the dead followed by the quick, who wept and wailed and filled the ether with crying and lament.

The procession reached the burial ground. The priests prayed and made incense, and the musicians blew upon their trumpets. Others spoke and praised the departed with fine words. Poets lamented him in their choicest verses. All this took a long and wearisome time. After a while the crowd dispersed and left the tombstone in whose fashioning sculptor had vied with mason. Around it were placed flowers arranged cunningly by artful hands. Then the cortege returned to the city, whilst I looked on from afar, thinking.

The sun inclined toward the west, and the shadow of rocks and trees lengthened and Nature began to shed her garments of light.

On that very moment I looked and beheld two men bearing a wooden casket. Behind them came a woman in rags carrying a suckling child. By her side trotted a dog, looking now at her, now at the

16

casket. It was the funeral procession of a poor man, a humble man. There went a wife shedding tears of grief and a child who wept at his mother's weeping, and a faithful dog in whose steps were a pain and a sadness.

They came to the burial ground and laid the coffin in a grave dug in a corner far from those marble headstones. Then they returned in silence, the while the dog looked back at the last resting place of his good companion. And so till they vanished from my sight beyond the trees.

And I looked toward the City of the Living, saying within myself: "That belongs to the wealthy and the mighty." And toward the City of the Dead I said: "This too belongs to the wealthy and the mighty. Where then, O Lord, is the home of the poor and the weak?"

Having thus spoken, I lifted my eyes to the clouds, whose edges were colored with gold by the rays of the setting sun. And a voice within me said: "Yonder."

THE POET'S DEATH IS HIS LIFE

Night spread its wings over the city, and the snow clothed it with a garment, and the cold drove men from the market places to take refuge in their dwellings. The wind rose sighing among the houses like a mourner who stands amidst tombstones lamenting the dead.

On the outskirts of that city was an old house with crumbling walls upon which the weight of the snows lay so that it was near falling. And in a corner of that house was a broken-down bed upon which lay a dying man, who watched the feeble light of a lamp battling with the darkness. He was a youth in the springtime of life who knew that the hour of his deliverance from the bonds of existence was at hand. So was he awaiting Death's coming. On his wan features was the light of hope and upon his lips a sad smile.

A poet he was who had come to rejoice the hearts of men with his beautiful sayings. Now he lay dying of hunger in the city of the living and the rich. A noble spirit that had descended by the grace of the gods to render life sweet was now bidding farewell to our world ere mankind had smiled on that spirit.

He was drawing his last breath and there was none by his side save the lamp, which was his companion in his aloneness, and scraps of paper on which were images to his gentle spirit.

The dying youth gathered together the remnants of his ebbing strength; he raised his hands heavenward and moved his withered eyelids as though his departing sight would pierce the roof of that broken-down hut so that he might look on the stars beyond the clouds. And he said:

"Come now, fair death, for my spirit yearns toward you. Come nigh and loose the fetters of matter, for I am become weary of their dragging. Come then, sweet death, and deliver me from men, who reckon me a stranger in their midst because I did speak the tongue of the angels in the language of mankind. Hasten, for men have rejected me and cast me into the corners of forgetfulness because I coveted not wealth as did they, nor profited from him who was weaker than I. Come to me, sweet death, and take me, for those of my kind need me not. Clasp me to your breast, which is full with love; kiss my lips, the lips that tasted not of a mother's kiss, nor touched a sister's cheek, nor felt a sweetheart's mouth. Hasten and embrace me, death, my beloved."

Then at the bedside of that dying youth stood the image of a woman of unearthly beauty. She was clothed in a garment white as snow and in her hand was a crown of lilies from heavenly valleys.

She drew near to him and embraced him, and closed his eyes that he might behold her with eyes of his spirit. She kissed his lips with a kiss of love, a kiss that left upon his lips a smile of fulfillment. And on that moment the hut became empty save of earth and pieces of paper scattered in dark corners.

The ages passed and the people of that city remained in the stupor of ignorance and folly. When they awoke therefrom and their eyes beheld the dawn of knowledge, they set up in the center of the town a great statue to the poet, and at an appointed time each year they held a festival in his honor.

How foolish are men!

DAUGHTERS OF THE SEA

In the depths of the ocean that surrounds the isles near the sun's rising-place was the dead body of a youth. Around him, among the coral plants, sat the golden-haired daughters of the sea gazing on him through their beautiful blue eyes. They spoke softly in tones of music, and their words were taken up by the deep and borne by the waves to the shore, whence the breeze carried them to my spirit's hearing.

Said the first one:

"This is a human who came down yesterday when the sea was angry."

And a second one said:

"Nay, the sea was not angry. But this man — such are called those descended from the gods — was in a war in which much blood was shed until the water became the color of red. This human is a victim of that war."

Said a third:

"I know not what war means, but I know that man was not satisfied with his conquest of the dry land but coveted the lordship of the oceans and invented strange machines to cleave the waters. Then Neptune, god of the seas, came to know, and he was angry because of this enmity. And man was made to appease our sovereign with sacrifices and offerings. That which we beheld yesterday descending was man's latest offering to mighty Neptune."

A fourth one said:

"How great is Neptune, but how hard is his heart! If I were mistress of the seas I would not be pleased with bloody sacrifices. Come, let us look on this dead youth; mayhap we learn something of humankind."

Then the daughters of the sea drew near to the body and searched in the pockets of his garment. In the garment nearest his heart was a letter, which one of them took and read:

"My darling. Midnight has struck and I keep vigil sleepless, with no one to console me save my tears and no body to comfort me but my hope in your return to me from the terrors of war. Well do I recall what you did tell me when we parted, that with every man are tears as a trust that must be returned one day.

"I know not, my love, what I write; rather shall I let my soul flow onto the paper. A soul tormented

22

by misery and consoled by love, which makes suffering a delight and grief a joy.

"When love made one our two hearts and we awaited the union of two bodies within which was one spirit, war called you and you followed it, impelled by duty to your country. Yet what thing is this duty that separates lovers and makes of women widows and of children orphans? What thing is this patriotism which for little causes calls to war to lay in ruins the land? What is this duty that fastens itself upon the wretched villages, but is heeded not by the strong and privileged?

"If duty exiles peace from among nations, and patriotism makes havoc of man's tranquillity, then away with duty and patriotism! . . . No, my darling, heed not my words, but be brave and a lover of your land. Do not hearken to the words of a woman whom love has blinded, whom separation has robbed of seeing. . . . If love brings you not back to me in this life, then love will join me with you in the life to come."

The sea maidens put back the letter beneath the youth's garments and swam away in silent grief. And when they were gone a distance, one of them said:

"In truth man's heart is harder than Neptune's."

THE SPIRIT

And the God of gods separated a Spirit from Himself and created in it Beauty.

He gave to it the lightness of the breeze at dawn and the fragrance of the flowers of the field and the softness of moonlight.

Then He gave to it a cup of joy, saying:

"You shall not drink of it except that you forget the Past and heed not the Future."

And He gave to it a cup of sadness, saying:

"You shall drink and know therefrom the meaning of Life's rejoicing."

Then He put therein a Love that would forsake it with the first sigh of satisfaction; and a Sweetness that would go out therefrom with the first word uttered.

And He caused to descend upon it knowledge from the heavens to guide it in the way of Truth. And planted in its depths Sight, that it might see the unseen.

Therein He created Feeling to flow with images and phantom forms;

And clothed it with a garment of Yearning woven by angels from rainbow strands.

In it He did put the darkness of Confusion, which is Light's image.

And the God took Fire from Wrath's furnace, and a Wind from the desert of Ignorance, and Sand from the seashore of Selfishness, and Earth from beneath the feet of the ages, and He created man.

He gave to him unseeing Force to rise up in fury with madness and subside before lust.

And the God of gods smiled and wept and knew a Love boundless and without limit, and He mated Man with his Spirit.

A SMILE AND A TEAR

The sun gathered up its garments from over those verdant gardens, and the moon rose from beyond the horizon and spilled its soft light over all. I sat there beneath a tree watching the changing shades of evening. I looked beyond the boughs to the stars scattered like coins upon a carpet of blue color, and I heard from afar the gentle murmur of the streams in the valley.

When the birds had made themselves safe in the leafy branches, and the flowers closed their eyes, and peace reigned, there came to my ears the fall of light footsteps on the grass. I turned my head and beheld a youth and a maid coming toward me. They stopped and sat them down at the foot of a tree.

The youth looked about him on all sides and said:

"Sit by me, beloved, and hear well my words. Smile, for your smiling is a sign to what is before us. Rejoice, for the very days rejoice for our sake. Yet does my soul tell me that your heart is full with doubting, and doubting in things of love is a sin.

"In days to come will you be mistress over these spacious lands which the moon lights up with its light; and lady of this palace which is likened to the palaces of kings. My fine horses will carry you to pleasure places, and my carriages will take you to merrymaking and dancing.

"Smile, my loved one, even as smiles the gold in my coffers. Look on me as do my father's precious stones Hearken to me, my love, for my heart longs only to pour its secret before you. Before us lies one year of bliss; a year we shall pass with gold in the palaces of the Nile; beneath the cedars of Lebanon. You shall meet with daughters of princes and nobles and they shall envy you your dress and adornments. All that shall I give you. Does it not find favor in your sight? Ah, how sweet is your smiling, for it is as the smile of my destiny."

After a while they departed, walking slowly and treading underfoot the flowers as the foot of the rich treads upon the heart of the poor. And so they vanished from my sight, the while I thought upon the place of riches in love; I thought upon riches, the source of men's evil; and love, the spring of light and happiness.

I fell to roaming the realms of thought, when of a sudden my eyes alighted on two figures that passed before me and sat them down on the grass. A youth and a maid who were come from a corner of the field where are the peasants' huts.

After a silence that was felt, I heard these words come forth with deep sighing from wounded lips:

"Dry your tears, my darling, for love, which has opened our eyes and made us its servants, will grant us the blessing of patience and forbearance. Dry your tears and be consoled, for we have made a covenant with love, and for that love shall we bear the torment of poverty and the bitterness of misfortune and the pain of separation.

"I shall not cease to contend with the days until I have wrested from them treasure worthy for your hands to receive. Love, which is God, will accept from us these tears and sighs as an offering, and we shall be rewarded in the measure of our due. Fare you well, my love, for I go ere the moon wanes."

Then I heard a soft voice in which was a sob; the voice of a virgin maid in which were the warmth of love and the bitterness of parting and the sweetness of patience, saying: "Farewell, beloved."

They separated, what time I remained sitting beneath that tree. And compassion's fingers drew me, and the secrets of this wondrous creation made me part. Upon that hour I looked toward Nature aslumber and pondered and found therein a thing boundless and without end. A thing not purchased with gold. I found a thing that is not effaced by autumn's tears nor destroyed by grief and wretchedness. A thing that endures and lives in the spring and comes to fruit in summer days. Therein I found Love.

A VISION

There in the midst of a field on the banks of a limpid stream I saw a cage whose bars were wrought by a cunning hand. In one corner of the cage was a dead bird and in another corner was a vessel wherein the water was dried up and a plate empty of seeds.

I stood, overcome by the silence, and listened humbly, as though in the dead bird and the voice of the stream were a sermon seeking out the heart and asking of the conscience. I pondered and considered and then I knew that the poor bird had died of thirst by the side of running water and perished of hunger in the midst of fields, the very cradle of life. Like a rich man locked in his treasury who dies of hunger in the midst of his gold.

And after a while I saw that the cage was become the dry skeleton of a man, and the dead bird was turned into a human heart; and in the heart a deep wound from which dripped blood. The edges of the wound were like to the lips of a grieving woman.

Then I heard a voice arising from the wound saying: "I am the human heart, the captive of matter and the slain of men's edicts. In the midst of this field of beauty on these banks of the source of life I am captive in this cage of laws fashioned by men for the feeling.

"In the cradle of Creation's beauties, between the hands of Love, I died neglected. For the bounty of those beauties and the fruits of this Love were forbidden to me. All that did awaken my desire was in man's conception shameful; and that for which I yearned did he judge a thing of scorn.

"I am the human heart, which is imprisoned in the darkness of the multitude's edicts and fettered by illusion until I am arrived at death's point.

"I am forsaken and abandoned in the corners of civilization and its seduction. The tongue of mankind is bound and its eyes are dry the while they smile."

These words did I hear and behold as they came out with the very drops of blood from that wounded heart.

Thereafter I saw no thing more, neither did I hear a voice, for I had returned to my reality.

LETTERS OF FIRE

"Here lies one whose name was writ in water."

JOHN KEATS

Is it that the nights pass by us
And destiny treads us underfoot?
Is it thus the ages engulf us and remember us not
    save as a name upon a page writ in water in
    place of ink?
Is this life to be extinguished
And this love to vanish
And these hopes to fade?

Shall death destroy that which we build
And the winds scatter our words,
And darkness hide our deeds?

Is this then life?
A past that has gone and left no trace,
A present, pursuing the past?
Or a future, without meaning, save when it is pres-
    ent and past?
Shall all that is joy in our hearts

32

And all that saddens our spirit
Vanish ere we know their fruits?

Shall man be even as the foam
That sits an instant on the ocean's face
And is taken by the passing breeze —
And is no more?

No, in truth, for the verity of life is life;
Life whose birth is not in the womb
Nor its end in death.

What are these years if not an instant in eternity?

This earthly life and all therein
Is but a dream by the side of the awakening
   We call by death and terror.
A dream, yet all we see and do therein
Endures with God's enduring.

The air bears every smile and every sigh
Arising from our hearts,
And stores away the voice of every kiss
Whose source and spring is love
And angels make account
Of every tear dropped by sadness from our eyes,
And fill the ears of wandering spirits
With song created by our hidden joys.

Yonder in the hereafter
We shall see the beating of our hearts
And comprehend the meaning of our godlike state,
That in this day we hold as nought
Because despair is ever at our heels.

The erring that today we call a weakness
Shall appear on the morrow
A link in man's existence.
The fret and toil that requite us not
Shall abide with us to tell our glory.
The afflications that we bear
Shall be to us a crown of honor.

If that sweet singer Keats had known that his songs
would never cease to plant the love of beauty in
men's hearts, surely he had said:

"Write upon my gravestone: Here lie the remains
of him who wrote his name on heaven's face in letters of fire."

AMIDST THE RUINS

The moon drew a fine veil across the City of the Sun and stillness enveloped all creation. And the awesome ruins rose like giants mocking at nocturnal things.

In that hour two forms without substance appeared out of the void like mist ascending from the surface of a lake. They sat them on a marble column which time had wrenched from that wondrous edifice, and looked down upon a scene that spoke of enchanted places. After a while one of them lifted up his head and, in a voice likened to the echo thrown back by distant valleys, said:

"These are the remains of those shrines that I builded for you, my beloved; and there the ruins of a palace I raised for your pleasure. Now they are level with the earth, and naught remains save a trace to tell to the nations of the glory for whose renown I expended my life and the might for whose aggrandizement I did put to work the weak. Look well and ponder, beloved, for the elements have vanquished the city I builded, and the ages have made as naught the wisdom I knew, and forgetfulness has overtaken the kingdom I founded. No thing remains save the particles of love created by your beauty and the beauty your love brought to life.

"I builded a temple in Jerusalem to worship therein. The priests sanctified it, and the days brought it to dust. Then I builded to love a temple within me, and God sanctified it, and no thing shall prevail against it. I passed my days seeking to know things of matter and substance, and men said: 'How wise is he in things of the world!' And the angels said: 'How little of wisdom is he!' Then did I behold you, beloved, and sang the song of love and yearning, and the angels rejoiced thereat, but as for men, they did not heed.

"The days of my splendor were as fences between my thirsting soul and the spirit that is in all creatures. And with my beholding you, love did awake and destroy the fences and I grieved over the days passed in submission to waves of despair, deeming all things under the sun a vanity. I put on my armor and took up my shield, and the tribes feared me. And when love lighted me I was humbled even before my kind. And when Death came, it put away that coat of mail and the earth and bore my love to God."

36

After a silence the other form spoke and said: "As the flower takes its fragrance and life from the soil, so in like measure does the spirit distill from the frailty of matter and its erring wisdom and strength."

Then the two forms were joined one with the other and became one and departed.

After a while the air spoke these words into those places:

"The Infinite keeps naught save Love, for it is in its own likeness."

A VISION

(*To the Viscountess S. L.
in answer to a letter she wrote me*)

Youth walked before me and I followed in his steps until we came to a distant field. There he stopped and stood, looking at the clouds drifting across the evening sky like a flock of white lambs. He looked at the trees whose naked branches pointed heavenward as if they would ask of heaven the return of their verdant leaves. And I said: "Where are we, youth?"

He replied: "We are in the fields of perplexity. Take heed."

"Let us then return, for the desolation of this place makes me afraid and the sight of the clouds and the naked trees saddens my spirit.

And he said: "Wait awhile, for perplexity is the beginning of knowledge."

Then I looked and beheld a nymph drawing nigh to us like a vision, and in my astonishment I cried: "Who is this?"

38

" 'Tis Melpomene, daughter of Jupiter, and goddess of tragedy," answered he.

"And what wants tragedy of me whilst you are yet by my side, happy youth?" And he answered me and said: "She has come to show you the world and its sorrows, for who has not seen sorrow cannot see joy."

Then the nymph put her hand over my eyes, and when she lifted it my youth was gone and I was naked of the garments of matter. And I said: "Where is youth, daughter of the gods?" She answered me not, but embraced me with her wings and took me in flight to the summit of a high mountain. And I saw the earth and all in it spread out before me like a page, and the secrets of its habitants appeared before my eyes like writings. And so did I stand in awe by the side of the nymph, gazing on Man's mysteries and striving to know life's symbols.

I saw, yea, I saw, yet would that I had been sightless. I saw angels of happiness contending with devils of misfortune, between them Man, and in his perplexity was he drawn now to hope, now to despair. I beheld love and hate playing with the human heart. This one concealed his guilt and made him drunk of the wine of submission and loosed his tongue in eulogy and praise. That one excited his passions and blinded him to truth and closed his ears against right speech.

39

I beheld the city squatting like a daughter of the streets holding to the hem of Man's garment. And the beautiful wild parts I saw standing from afar and weeping for his sake.

I beheld priests, sly like foxes; and false messiahs dealing in trickery with the people. And men crying out, calling upon wisdom for deliverance, and Wisdom spurning them with anger because they heeded not when she called them in the streets before the multitude.

I saw heads of religion vying one with another in raising their eyes heavenward, the while their hearts were interred in the graves of lust. I saw young men showing love on their tongues and drawing near to the hopes of their boldness, their divineness a distant thing, and their affections aslumber.

I saw also lawmakers trading their garbled speech in the market of shame and deceit; and physicians making sport with the trusting souls of the simple. The ignorant sitting with the wise also did I see, raising his past upon a throne of glory and cushioning his present at ease upon a carpet of spaciousness and spreading for his future a bed of honor.

I saw the wretched poor sowing and the powerful rich harvesting and eating; and oppression standing there and the people calling it Law.

Thieves and robbers and darkness I beheld, stealing the treasures of the mind; and the custodians of light drowned in the sleep of sloth.

A woman I saw like a lute in the hands of one who cannot play upon it and is displeased with its sound.

I beheld those armies investing the city of privilege; and armies in retreat because they were few in number and not united. And true freedom walking alone in the streets, seeking shelter before doors and rejected by the people. Then I saw selffulness walking in a mighty procession and the multitude hailed it as freedom.

I saw religion buried within books and in its stead illusion. I saw men wearing patience as a cloak for cowardice and calling forbearance by the name of sloth; and gentleness they dubbed as fear. I saw the intruder at the banquet making claim while the guest remained silent. And wealth in the hands of a squanderer as a snare of evildoing, and in the hands of the miser as hatred of his fellows. In the hands of the sage I saw not any riches.

When I beheld all these things I cried out in agony: "Is this, then, the earth, daughter of the gods? Is this indeed man?"

And she answered in a still wounding voice: "This is the path of the spirit, paved with stones and thorns. This is man's shadow. This is the night, but morning will come."

Thereupon she put her hands on my eyes, and when they were lifted I beheld myself and my youth walking slowly. And hope ran before me.

TODAY AND YESTERDAY

The rich man walked in the garden of his palace, and in his footsteps followed care and above his head hovered disquiet like vultures that circle over a dead body. He came to a lake that men had wrought with art and cunning, and around it were images in alabaster. Then he sat him down and looked, now at the water pouring forth from the mouths of the stone figures as the pouring out of thoughts from the imagination of a lover; now at his fine palace, sitting on high ground like a mole on the cheek of a maiden.

There he sat, and remembrance sat beside him unfolding before his eyes pages that the past had written in the story of his life. And he fell to reading, the while tears concealed from his sight that which men had builded about him, and grief brought back to his heart the strands of days that the gods had woven, and his anguish overflowed in words and he said:

42

"Yesterday I pastured my sheep on the green heights and rejoiced in life and played on my pipe to tell of my rejoicing. Today I am the captive of greed, and riches are leading me to riches, and more riches to miserliness, and miserliness to despair. I was as a bird trilling its song and a butterfly fluttering hither and thither. No gentle breeze was lighter in step on the flower-tops than my footsteps upon those fields.

"Behold me now a prisoner of people's customs. See how I dissimulate in my dress and at my board and in all that I do for the sake of people's favor and approbation. Would that I were born to rejoice in existence! Riches have decreed me tread the paths of sorrow, and I am like to a camel heavy-laden with gold and dying beneath its burden.

"Where are the vast plains and the murmuring brooks? Where the washed air and nature's glory? Where is my Godlikeness? All these things are lost to me, and naught remains save the gold I love ever mocking me, an abundance of slaves, and diminished joy; and a mansion I raised to bring down my happy state.

"Once I roamed with the Bedouin's daughter, with virtue as a third one and love as our companion and the moon our guardian. This day do I walk among women whose necks are outstretched, in whose eyes is dalliance, who sell for rings and girdles and bracelets their bodies.

43

"Once I played with young playmates and we ran among the trees like gazelles. We sang together songs of happiness and shared the pleasures of field and meadow. Today am I become a lamb in the midst of ravening beasts. Whensoever I walk in the streets eyes of hate are cast upon me and envious fingers point to me. And in the pleasure grounds I see but frowning faces and lifted heads.

"Yesterday was I granted life and nature's beauty; today I am plundered of them: yesterday was I rich in my joy; today I am become poor in my riches. Yesterday I was with my flock as a merciful ruler among his subjects; today I stand before gold as a cringing slave before a tyrannous master.

"I knew not that riches would efface the very essence of my spirit, nor did I know that wealth would lead it to the dark caves of ignorance. And I reckoned not that what people call glory is naught except torment and the pit."

And the man of riches rose from his place and walked slowly toward his palace, sighing the while, and saying again and again: "Are these, then, riches? Is this, then, the god whose priest I am become? Is this the thing we barter for life, yet cannot exchange it for a single grain of life? Who will sell me one beautiful thought for a measure of gold? Who will take from me a handful of gems for a particle of love? Who will give me an eye through which to behold beauty and take in its stead my treasury?"

And when he came to the gate of his palace he turned and looked toward the city as did Jeremiah to Jerusalem. He raised his hands toward it as though in lamentation and cried out in a loud voice: "O people who walk in darkness and sit in the shadow of death; who pursue woe and judge falsely and speak in ignorance! Till when will you eat of thistles and thorns and cast fruits and herbs into the abyss? Till when will you dwell in wild and desolate places and turn aside from the garden of life? Wherefore do you clothe yourselves in rags and tatters when garments of silk are fashioned for you?

"O people, the lamp of wisdom is extinguished; therefore replenish it with oil. And the wayfarer destroys the vineyard of good fortune; therefore watch over it. The robber plunders the coffers of your peace; therefore take heed."

In that minute a poor man stood before the rich man and stretched forth his hand for alms. The rich man looked on him, and his trembling lips became firm and his sad countenance expanded and from his eyes shone the light of kindliness. The yesterday he had lamented on the shore of the lake was come today to greet him. He drew near to the beggar and kissed him with a kiss of love and brotherliness and

45

filled his hands with gold. Then he said with compassion in his words: "Take now, my brother, and return on the morrow with your companions and take you all of what is yours." And the poor man smiled the smile of a withered flower after the rain and departed hastily.

Then the man of riches entered into his palace, saying: "All things in life are good, even riches, for they teach man a lesson. Riches are as a musical instrument that gives off only discord to him who cannot play on it. Wealth is as love in that it destroys him who withholds it but grants life to him who gives freely of it."

HAVE MERCY, MY SOUL

How long, my soul, will you continue in lamenting
Whilst yet sensible of my weakness?
Until when will you cry out,
Whilst yet I have naught save the speech of men
To tell therein your dreams?

Consider, my soul,
How I did pass my days in hearkening to your
    teaching.
Look well, my tormentor, behold my body
Wasted and enfeebled in pursuit of you.
My heart was sovereign,
It is now become your slave;
My patience was a comforter,
It is now my chastiser.
My youth was to me a fellow,
Yet today is become my blamer.
This is the all the gods have granted.
What thing more do you desire!

I have denied myself
And abandoned life's joy,
And turned aside from the glory of my years.
Now naught remains to me save you.
Judge me, then, with justice,
For justice is your splendor,
Or summon Death, and free me
From the prison of your essence.

Have mercy, my soul,
For you have burdened me
With a love I cannot carry.
You and love are as one in strength,
And I and matter — weakness divided.
Shall the struggle between strong and weak be eter-
    nal?

Have mercy, my soul,
For you did show to me fortune from afar.
You and fortune are upon a high mountain;
I and misfortune in a deep valley.
Shall the high and the low meet?

Have mercy, my soul,
For you have revealed to me beauty —
And concealed it.
You and beauty are in the light;
I and ignorance in darkness.
Shall light and darkness merge?

You, O soul, rejoice in the hereafter —
Ere its coming.
This body despairs of life
Whilst yet in life.

You walk toward the Infinite, hastening;
This body falters in its step to destruction.
You tarry not, and it does not hasten.
This, O soul, is the summit of despair.
You are raised aloft by Heaven;
This body falls, descending with earth's pull.
You do not console it,
And it says you not: "Well done."
This, my soul, is hate.

You, O soul, are rich in your wisdom;
This body is poor in its understanding.
You deal not with leniency,
And it follows you not.
This, my soul, is the sum of wretchedness.

You walk in the still night
To the beloved,
And rejoice in his embrace and love.
This body remains
E'er the slain of separation and longing.
Have mercy on me, my soul.

THE WIDOW AND HER SON

Night descended swiftly upon northern Lebanon, overtaking a day wherein much snow had fallen on the villages around Wadi Kadisha.* It made of the fields and hillocks a white page upon which the winds had inscribed lines and then erased them. The tempest played with them, making the angry sky at one with wrathful nature.

People took refuge in their houses and beasts in their stalls, and no living thing moved. No thing remained without save the bitter cold and the black terrifying night, and death, strong and fearsome.

In a lonely cottage in one of those villages a woman sat before the fire weaving a garment of wool. By her side sat her only child, looking now into the fire, now up at the serene face of his mother.

In that hour the storm grew in force and the winds increased in violence until the walls of the

* I.e., the Valley of the Saints. So called because it was a refuge of ascetics and holy men seeking sanctuary from the world and its tribulations. — Author's note.

house trembled and shook. The boy became frightened and drew near to his mother, seeking in her tenderness a protection against the enraged elements. She held him to her breast and kissed him and seated him on her lap, saying: "Be not afraid, my son, for it is naught save Nature warning man of her might against his littleness, and her strength by the side of his weakness. Fear not, my child, for beyond the falling snows and thick clouds and the howling tempest is a Holy Spirit who is knowing of the needs of the fields. Beyond all things is a Power that looks upon the wretchedness of mankind with mercy and compassion. Be not frightened, my precious one, for Nature, who smiles with the spring and laughs on a summer's day and sighs with autumn's coming, now wants to weep. With her cold tears is watered sleeping life under the layers of earth.

"Sleep, then, my child, for your father looks down upon us from eternal pastures. Storm and snow bring near to us the remembrance of those immortal spirits.

"Sleep, my darling, for out of the warring elements will come forth beautiful flowers for you to gather in the mouth of Nisan.* So it is, my son, that men reap not love save after painful absence and bitter patience and black despair.

"Sleep, my little one, and sweet dreams shall

* April.

51

come to your spirit, unafraid of the awe of night and the cold without."

The boy looked up at his mother with eyes darkened by sleepiness and said: "My eyes are sleepy, Mother, and I am afraid to go to sleep before saying my prayers."

The mother embraced him tenderly and, looking through her tears to his child's face, said:

"Say with me, my child: Have mercy, O Lord, upon the poor and guard them against the bitter cold and clothe their naked bodies with Thy hands. Look Thou to the orphans aslumber in huts, whose bodies are hurt by the snow's cold breath.

"Hearken, O Lord, to the cry of the widow standing in the street between death and cold. Stretch forth Thy hand to the rich man's heart and open Thou his eyes that he may see the wretchedness of the weak and the oppressed.

"Show pity, O Lord, to those ahunger outside doors on this dark night, and guide the stranger to a refuge of warmth, and have mercy on his strangeness.

"Look, O Lord, upon the fledgling and preserve with Thy right hand the tree fearful of the harsh wind. Be this so, O Lord."

And when sleep had gathered up the boy, his mother laid him upon the bed and kissed his brow with trembling lips. Then she returned to the fireside and there sat making for him a coat of wool.

52

A PEOPLE AND DESTINY

At the foot of Mount Lebanon a shepherdess sat by a stream that wound its way among rocks like a silver thread. About her moved her flock of sheep, lean and sickly of body, feeding off the dried-up grass that grew amidst clumps of thistle and thorn. A maiden she was, looking into the twilight as though she would read in it of days to come on the pages of space. Tears stood in her eyes like dewdrops on the narcissus, and sorrow opened her lips that it might plunder her heart of sighs.

And when evening came and the heights were clothed in garments of black, there appeared unawares before the girl an old man whose white hair fell upon his shoulders and breast. In his right hand was a sharpened scythe. He spoke with a voice that had in it the sound of sea waves, saying: "Peace be upon Syria."

The girl rose to her feet, afraid, and said in a voice in which were fear and grief:

53

"What would you of me, Destiny? Behold the remnant of a flock that once filled these valleys; the remnant of your coveting. Are you come, then, to demand even more? These are the pastures your treading has rendered barren; once they were the source of sustenance and fertility. My lambs fed of the flower-tops and gave forth sweet milk. Now are their bellies empty and they gnaw thistles and tree roots out of fear that they might perish.

"Fear God, Destiny, and get you hence from me, for the remembrance of your oppression has made me to hate life, and the cruelty of your scythe has made death beloved of me.

"Leave me with my aloneness to drink of tears for wine and lift my nostrils to grief as a breeze. Go you to the places of the West wherein the people are at life's wedding feast and let me to mourn at burials you have determined."

The old man looked on her as a father looks on his child. Then he concealed his scythe in the folds of his cloak and said:

"Naught have I taken from you, O Syria, save of my gifts; neither have I plundered, but have borrowed to restore. Know that your sisters the nations have a portion in that splendor which was your handmaid, and title to wear the cloak that was yours. I and justice are the two elements of one being. It is not pleasing to me that I give not to your sisters that which I gave to you. I am not able to make you equal portions in my love, for love does not so divide itself. Your likeness is in your neighbors, Egypt and Persia and Greece, for their flocks are even as your flocks, and their pastures even as your pastures. That which you call by abasement, O Syria, is in my sight a needful slumber before the awakening to strength and deeds. No flower returns to life save by way of death, and love does not become a mighty thing except after separation."

The old man drew near to the girl and, stretching forth his hand, said: "Take you my hand, Daughter of the Prophets." And she took his hand and looked toward him through a veil of tears, saying: "Fare you well, Destiny, fare you well." And he returned: "Fare you well, Syria, for we shall meet again."

Whereupon the old man was gone with the quickness of lightning. The shepherdess called to her flock and went on her way, murmuring the while: "Shall there again be meeting?"

BEFORE THE THRONE
OF BEAUTY

I fled from the multitude and wandered in that wide valley, now following the course of the stream, now listening to the conversation of the birds, until I came to a place guarded by branches from the heat of the sun. There I sat and communed with my spirit and addressed my aloneness. A thirsty spirit that saw the visible as a mirage and the unseen as an oasis.

And when my mind had fled from the prison of matter to the realm of imagining, I turned my head and beheld, standing by my side, a maiden. It was a nymph of paradise. On her was neither garment nor adornment save a branch of the vine that concealed part of her, and a crown of poppies that bound her hair of gold. And when she perceived my glances of surprise and wonderment, she said: "I am a daughter of the forests. Fear me not."

And I asked her, saying: "Do those of your like dwell in a place inhabited by desolation and wild beasts? Tell me who you are and whence you come."

She sat down on the grass and said: "I am a symbol of Nature. I am the virgin whom your forefathers did adore; for whom they builded altars and shrines and temples in Baalbek and Aphaca and Byblos." And I said: "Those temples are destroyed and the bones of my forefathers lie level with the earth, and naught remains of their gods and their ways save a few pages between the covers of books."

Said she: "Many of their gods live in the life of their adorers and die in their death. Others of them live eternally and forever. My god-state is sustained by the beauty you behold wheresoever you lift your eyes; a beauty that is Nature in all her forms. A beauty that is the beginning of the shepherd's happiness as he stands among the hills; and of the villager's in his fields; and of the wandering tribes between mountain and plain. A beauty that is a stepping-stone for the wise to the throne of living truth."

Then I said, the while my heartbeats uttered things unknown of the tongue: "In truth, beauty is a terrible and awe-filling force." And on her lips was the smile of a flower and in her eyes the hidden things of life. She said: "You, children of the flesh, are afraid of all things, even yourselves do you fear. You fear heaven, the source of safety. Nature do you fear, yet it is a haven of rest. You fear the God of all gods, and attribute to Him envy and malice. Yet what is He if not love and compassion?"

After a silence, in which were gentle dreams, I asked of her: "What thing is this beauty? For people differ in its defining and their knowledge thereof as they contend one with another in praise and love of it."

And she answered: "It is that which draws your spirit. It is that which you see and makes you to give rather than receive. It is that thing you feel when hands are stretched forth from your depths to clasp it to your depths. It is that which the body reckons a trial and the spirit a bounty. It is the link between joy and sorrow. It is all that you perceive hidden and know unknown and hear silent. It is a force that begins in the holy of holies of your being and ends in that place beyond your visions. . . ."

Then the daughter of the forests drew near to me and laid her fragrant hand on my eyelids. And when she lifted it, behold, I was alone in that valley.

I returned, the while my spirit recited: "In truth is beauty that which you see and makes you to give rather than receive."

A VISIT FROM WISDOM

In the stillness of night Wisdom came and stood by my bed. She gazed upon me like a tender mother and wiped away my tears, and said: "I have heard the cry of your spirit and I am come to comfort it. Open your heart to me and I shall fill it with light. Ask of me and I shall show you the way of truth."

And I said: "Who am I, Wisdom, and how came I to this frightening place? What manner of things are these mighty hopes and these many books and strange patterns? What are these thoughts that pass as doves in flight? And these words composed by desire and sung by delight, what are they? What are these conclusions, grievous and joyous, that embrace my spirit and envelop my heart? And those eyes which look at me seeing into my depths and fleeing from my sorrows? And those voices mourning my days and chanting my littleness, what are they?

"What is this youth that plays with my desires

and mocks at my longings, forgetful of yesterday's deeds, rejoicing in paltry things of the moment, scornful of the morrow's coming?

"What is this world that leads me whither I know not, standing with me in despising? And this earth that opens wide its mouth to swallow bodies and lets evil things to dwell on its breast? What is this creature that is satisfied with the love of fortune, whilst beyond its union is the pit? Who seeks Life's kiss whilst Death does smite him, and brings the pleasure of a minute with a year of repentance, and gives himself to slumber the while dreams call him? What is he who flows with the rivers of folly to the sea of darkness? O Wisdom, what manner of things are these?"

And she answered, saying:

"You would see, human creature, this world through the eyes of a god. And you would seek to know the secrets of the hereafter with the thinking of men. Yet in truth is this the height of folly.

"Go you to the wild places and you shall find there the bee above the flowers and behold the eagle swooping down on his prey. Go you into your neighbor's house and see then the child blinking at the firelight and his mother busied at her household tasks. Be you like the bee and spend not the days of spring looking on the eagle's doing. Be as the child and rejoice in the firelight and heed not your mother's affairs. All that you see with your eyes was and is for your sake.

"The many books and the strange patterns and beautiful thoughts are the shades of those spirits that came ere you were come. The words that you do weave are a bond between you and your brothers. The conclusions, grievous and joyous, are the seeds that the past did scatter in the field of the spirit to be reaped by the future. That youth who plays with your desires is he who will open the door of your heart to let enter the light. This earth with the ever open mouth is the savior of your spirit from the body's slavery. This world which walks with you is your heart; and your heart is all that you think that world. This creature whom you see as ignorant and small is the same who has come from God's side to learn pity through sadness, and knowledge by way of darkness."

Then Wisdom put her hand on my burning brow and said:

"Go then forward and do not tarry, for before walks perfection. Go, and have not fear of thorns on the path, for they deem naught lawful save corrupted blood."

THE TALE OF A FRIEND

I knew him as a young man lost on the road of Life, ruled by his youthful deeds, baiting Death in the pursuit of his desires. I knew him as a tender bloom borne by the winds of fancy to the fathomless sea of lust.

I knew him in that little village as a cruel boy whose fingers tore apart the nests of birds and slew their young. Who trampled flowers underfoot and destroyed their beauty. I knew him at school, as one in adolescence, scorning learning and an enemy of peace. I knew him in the city for a youth who traded his father's honor in the market place of loss, squandering his riches in places of shame and surrendering his mind to the daughter of the vine.

Withal, I loved him. Ay, I loved him with a love compounded of sorrow and kneaded with compassion. I loved him because his faults were not the fruits of a small spirit, but rather the acts of a spirit weak and despairing.

The spirit, O people, avoids the path of wisdom unwillingly, but returns thereto willingly. And in youth is a whirlwind that blows the dust and the sands and carries them along and fills the eye to close and blind it.

I loved that youth and felt for him a warmth, for I had seen the dove of his conscience contending with the vulture of his evil parts, and the dove was vanquished by her adversary's strength and not by cause of her cowardliness. The conscience is a judge, just and weak, and weakness stands in the way of its carrying out·of judgment.

I have said that I loved him. But love comes in many guises. Sometimes it is as wisdom, other times justice, ofttimes hope. My love for him was my hope that the strong light of its sun might triumph over the darkness of transient sorrows. But I knew not when and where a filthiness became a clean thing, and cruelty kindness, and ignorance wisdom. A man knows not in what manner the spirit is freed from matter until after it is freed. Neither knows he how a flower smiles save after the coming of morning.

2

The days followed on the heels of the nights, and I remembered that youth with pain and grief and I uttered his name with a sighing that rent the heart. Then yesterday came from him a letter, saying:

"Come to me, my friend, for I wish to take you to a young man. Your heart will rejoice at his meeting and your spirit will be refreshed at his knowing."

I said: "Alas! Does he seek to add to his sad friendship the companionship of another like him? Is he not in himself an example to point the words of error? Does he now seek to write in the margin of that example the words of his companions so that not even one letter in the book of matter shall pass me by?"

Again did I say: "I will go, and mayhap the spirit in its wisdom shall find for me a fig among the thistles, and the heart in its love draw light out of darkness."

And when night fell I betook myself thence and found the young man alone in a room reading from a book of verse. I greeted him and wondered at the book in his hands, and said:

"Where, then, is the new friend?"

"I am he, my friend, I am he," he returned. He sat with a quietness I had not known in him; then he looked at me. In his eyes was a strange light that pierced the breast. The eyes in which I had for so long seen no thing save harshness and cruelty now radiated a light that filled the heart with love. In a voice that seemed to come from another than him he said: "In truth, that one whom you knew as a child and whose playfellow you were and whom you accompanied in youth is dead, and out of his dying I am born. I am he, your new friend. Take, then, my hand."

I took his hand and felt in its touch a gentle spirit coursing with the blood; ay, that hard and cruel hand was become soft and tender. The fingers that yesterday were a panther's claws today caress the heart with their lightness.

Again I spoke (would that I remembered the strangeness of my words) : "Who are you, what has befallen you, how are you become thus? Has the Spirit taken you as a sanctuary and sanctified you, or are you playing before me a poet's fancy?"

He answered: "Ay, my friend, the Spirit has in truth descended upon me and sanctified me. A mighty love has made my heart an altar of purity. It is woman; woman, whom yesterday I reckoned a plaything of men, has delivered me from the darkness of the pit and opened before me the gates of paradise and I have entered. The true woman has led me to the Jordan of her love and baptized me. She whose sister I did in my folly despise has lifted me to the throne of glory. She whose companion in my blindness I despoiled has cleansed me with her love. She whose kind I did enslave has liberated me with her beauty. She that did cast the first man from the Garden by the strength of her desire and his weakness has led me back to Eden by her compassion and my obedience."

I looked on him in that moment and beheld tears in his eyes and a smile on his lips and the light of love as a crown on his head. I drew near to him and kissed his brow in blessing as the priest kisses the face of the altar.

I bade him farewell, repeating the while his words: "She that did cast the first man from the Garden by the strength of her desire and his weakness has led me back to Eden by her compassion and my obedience."

FANTASY AND TRUTH

Life carries us hither and thither and destiny moves us from one place to another. We see not save the obstacle set in our path; neither do we hear save a voice that makes us to fear.

Beauty appears before us seated on her throne of glory and we draw nigh. And in the name of longing do we defile her garment's hem and wrest from her the crown of purity.

Love passes by us clothed in a robe of gentleness, and we are afraid and hide us in dark caves, or follow her and do evil things in her name.

The wise man walks in our midst bearing his heavy yoke; yet is it softer than the breath of a flower and gentler than the breezes of Lebanon.

Wisdom stands on the street corner and calls to us above the multitude, but we deem her a thing without worth and despise them that follow her.

Wisdom summons us to her board that we may

67

enjoy her food and drink; and we go thence and fill our bellies, and that table becomes an occasion for littleness and a place of self-abasement.

Nature stretches forth to us the hand of friendship and bids us take delight in her beauty; but we fear her stillness and take refuge in the city and tumble one upon another as a flock of sheep before the prowling wolf.

Truth visits us led by the smile of a child and a lover's kiss, and we close the door of our tenderness against her and abandon her as one unclean.

The human heart asks succor of us, and the spirit calls us, but we stand as one turned to stone, hearing not nor understanding.

And when one hears the cry of his heart and the call of his spirit, we say that such a one is possessed of a madness, and we cleanse ourselves of him.

Thus wise pass the nights and we are heedless of them. The days meet us, and we fear the days and the nights.

We are near to earth, yet the gods are our kin. We pass by the bread of life, and hunger feeds off our strength.

How sweet to us is life, and how far we are from life!

O MY POOR FRIEND

O you who were born on a bed of sorrow and reared in the lap of misfortune and brought to manhood in the houses of oppression, you who eat your crust of bread with a sigh and drink of your clouded water with tears and weeping.

O soldier who is sentenced by man's cruel law to forsake his mate and his little ones and kin to go out of the field of death for the sake of greed in its guise of duty.

And you, poet, who sojourn in the land of your birth, unknown among those who know you, satisfied with a morsel and fragments of ink and paper.

O captive, cast into the darkness for a small wrong made big by those who match evil with evil; banished by them that seek doing good by way of corruption.

And you, unfortunate woman, on whom God did bestow beauty; upon whom the eyes of the young men of the age fell, who pursued you and tempted you and conquered your poverty with gold. To them you did yield and were left as prey trembling in the hold of misery and shame.

You, my beloved weak, are the martyrs of men's law. You are in despair, and your despairing is the fruit of the iniquity of the strong and the ruler's deceit and the rich man's oppressing, and the selffulness of the lustful.

Despair not. For beyond the wrongs of the world, beyond matter and clouds and air, beyond all things is a Power that is justice and mercy and love and compassion.

You are as flowers that grow in the shade. Gentle breezes shall pass and bear your needs to the sunlight, and you shall live there a pleasant life.

You are like to naked trees bowed under heavy winter snows. But soon will spring come to clothe you with fresh green leaves.

Truth shall tear aside the veil of tears that conceals your smile. And I will greet you, my brothers, and humble your oppressors.

LAMENT OF THE FIELD

At the hour of dawn, before the sun's rising from beyond the horizon, I sat in the middle of a field communing with Nature. At that hour filled with purity and beauty I lay on the grass, what time men were yet wrapped in slumber, disturbed now by dreams, now by awakening. I lay there seeking to know from all that I looked upon the truth of Beauty and the beauty of Truth.

And when my reflecting had set me apart from the flesh, and my imaginings lifted the covering of matter from off my inner self, I felt my spirit growing, drawing me near to Nature and revealing to me her hidden things and teaching me the language of her wonders.

Thus I was as the breeze passed through the branches of the tree, sighing plaintively like an orphan child. I sought understanding and said: "Why do you sigh, gentle breeze?" And it answered: "Because I am going to the city away from the sun's warmth. To the city, where the germs of sickness and disease will cling to the hem of my clean garment, and the poisoned breath of flesh breathe on me. Because of this do you behold my sadness."

Then I looked toward the flowers and saw dewdrops falling like tears from their eyes. I said:

"Why weep you thus, fair flowers?" And one of them lifted up its head in reply and said:

"We weep because men will come and cut off our heads and take us to the city and sell us, who are free, as slaves. And when evening falls and we are withered they will cast us into the dust. How then should we weep not when men in their cruelty would separate us from our home the field?"

After a while I heard the brook lamenting like a bereaved mother over her lost ones, and I asked: "Why do you lament, sweet brook?" And it answered: "Because I am driven to the city, wherein men despise me and exchange me for the juice of grapes and make me to carry their dregs. How then should I not lament when soon my innocence will become guilt and my purity dross?"

And I heard the birds chanting a mournful chant like to a dirge and I said: "Wherefor do you mourn, comely birds?" Whereupon a small one among them approached me and said: "Tomorrow a man will come bearing in his hand a fearful instrument to destroy us, as the sickle cuts off the standing corn. We shall bid farewell one of the other, for we

72

know not which among us will escape his doom. How then should we not mourn when death follows us wheresoever we go?"

The sun rose from behind a mountain and crowned the treetops with gold, the while I asked myself why men pull down what Nature has builded up.

THE PALACE AND THE HUT

Night was falling and the lights in the mansion of the rich man shone brightly. The servants, clad in velvet, with buttons gleaming on their breasts, stood awaiting the guests. Music played and the lords and ladies descended on that palace from all parts, drawn in their carriages by fine horses. There they entered, trailing after them their rich garments and dragging the ends of pomp and pride.

Then the men rose from their places and took the ladies to dance. And that hall became a garden through which the breezes of melody passed, and its flowers inclined in awe and wonder.

Soon midnight approached and the table was laid with the choicest of fruits and the finest of foods. Cups were passed from one to another and wine played with the senses of all those there until they in turn took to play. And when morning was near they dispersed, for they were tired with merrymaking and bemused by wine and wearied of dancing and revelry. And everyone betook himself to his bed.

2

As the sun sank low beyond the horizon, a man dressed in the garb of a laborer stood at the door of a mean house and knocked thereon. It opened to him and he entered, greeting those within with a cheerful countenance, and sat down in the midst of his children by the fire.

After a while his wife prepared a meal and they seated themselves around a wooden table and ate their food. And after their repast was finished they rose and sat by the lamp, which sent the arrows of its feeble yellow rays into the heart of the darkness. When the first watch of night was passed they lay down in silence and gave themselves to sleep.

At dawn's approach that poor man rose from his bed and partook of a little bread and milk with his wife and little ones. Then he kissed them and went away with a heavy spade over his shoulder to the field, to water it with his sweat and make it fruitful that it might feed those mighty ones who yestereve made merry.

The sun rose from beyond the mountain and the

heat was heavy on the head of the toiler, the while those with riches still slept in their mansions.

So is man's burden: a tragedy played on the stage of time. Many are the spectators that applaud; few are they that comprehend and know.

TWO INFANTS

A Prince stood on the balcony of his palace and hailed the multitude gathered in the palace garden and cried: "I bring you good tidings and felicitate our country, for the Princess has brought forth a boy to perpetuate the honor and glory of my line. He will be to you a pride and delight and the heir to the inheritance of my great forefathers. Rejoice then and give songs of praise, for your future now belongs to this scion of our house.

And the multitude raised its voice in shouting and filled the air with ululations of joy in honor of one to be reared in the cradle of plenty and raised in the seat of the mighty; to be supreme ruler over the necks of slaves and to drive with his strength the weak. To be free to enchain their bodies and destroy their souls. For such a thing were they rejoicing and singing songs and drinking out of cups of joy.

And that time the people of that town sang the praises of power and humbled themselves before an oppressor and made the angels to weep for their littleness, a woman lay prostrate on a bed of pain in an old and abandoned dwelling. To her burning breast she clasped an infant swaddled in rags. A girl she was to whom the days had allotted poverty and misery and whom men had forsaken. A wife whose man had the tyranny of the Prince destroyed. A woman alone to whom the gods that night had sent a little friend to shackle her hands against earning her substance by their labor.

When the noise of the multitude in the streets had died, the wretched woman placed the infant on her lap and looked into its shining eyes, and she wept a bitter weeping as though she would baptize the child with her tears. Then in a voice such as even would pierce a rock she said: "Why did you come, O flesh of my flesh, from the world of spirits? Was it out of desire to share with me life's bitterness? Or out of compensation for my weakness? Why did you leave the angels and the spaceless firmament for this life, narrow and full with misery and lowliness? I have naught but tears, my only one. Will they nurture you in place of milk? And will my naked arms clothe you instead of woven stuffs? The smallest of animals pasture on sweet grasses and take shelter in safety at night. The tiniest of birds pick up grain and sleep rejoicing in the branches. But for you, my child, there is naught save my sighing and my weakness."

Thus saying, she clasped the child closely to her breast, as though she would make the two bodies one, and lifted her eyes heavenward and cried: "Have compassion on us, O Lord!"

And when the clouds scattered, revealing the moon's face, the gentle rays entered through the window of that poor house and spilled themselves over two cold bodies.

UNDER THE SUN

"I have seen all the works that are done under the sun; and, behold, all is vanity and vexation of spirit."
ECCLESIASTES i, 14

O spirit of Solomon that floats in the vast spaces in the world of spirits, O you that have cast off the garments of matter, which we now do wear, you have left behind you these words born of weakness and despair which did create in the prisons of bodies weakness and despair.

Now is it known unto you that in this life is a meaning not concealed by death. Is it perchance that that knowledge, which is not understood until the spirit is freed from its earthly bonds, is withheld from mankind?

Now is it known unto you that life is not as a vexation of spirit, nor that all under the sun is in vain; but rather that all things were and are ever marching toward truth. Yet we have clung to your words and pondered deep on them and have not ceased to reckon them a shining wisdom. But they

80

are a darkness that loses the mind and obscures hope, and you are knowing of that.

Now is it known unto you that ignorance and evil and tyranny have good causes. And we see not beauty save in manifestations of wisdom and the results of virtue and the fruits of justice.

Well do you know that poverty and grief purify the human heart, and that our bounded minds see no free thing in life save happiness and ease.

Well do you know that the spirit is going toward the light in face of the obstacles of life, yet do we still recite your words which tell that man is naught but a plaything in the hand of a Force unknown.

You did repent of your sending abroad a spirit to weaken love of this life and destroy the passion for the life to come. Yet did we continue to treasure your words.

O spirit of Solomon, who dwell in the region of the immortals, inspire those who love wisdom so that they take not the path of despair and disbelief; mayhap it shall be an atonement for a sin not intended.

A GLIMPSE INTO
THE FUTURE

From beyond the wall of the Present I heard the praises of mankind.

I heard the voices of bells that shook the very air, heralding the commencement of prayer in the sanctuary of Beauty. Bells wrought by strength from the metal of feeling and raised above that holy shrine — the human heart.

From beyond the Future I saw the multitudes prostrate on Nature's breast, turning toward the rising sun, awaiting the morning light — the morning of Truth.

I beheld the city razed low, naught remaining of it save its ruins telling of the flight of Darkness before Light.

I saw old men seated beneath the poplar and the willow tree; around them stood boys listening to their tales of the times.

I saw young men playing on stringed instruments and the pipe; and maidens with loosed hair dancing around them under jasmine boughs.

Likewise did I see those in middle age gathering the harvest, and women bearing away the yield with songs of gladness and joy;

And a woman too I did see who cast forth her unseemly garment for a crown of lilies and a girdle of verdant leaves from off the tree.

I saw a companionship between man and all creation;

And flights of birds and butterflies drawing nigh to him in safety,

And gazelles flocking to the pool, trusting.

I looked, and beheld not poverty, neither did I see anything above what suffices. Rather did I meet brotherhood and equality.

I saw not any physician, for each morrow is a healer unto itself by the law of knowledge and experience.

Neither did I see a priest, for conscience was become the High Priest.

No lawyer did I behold, for Nature was risen among them as a tribunal recording covenants of amity and fellowship.

I saw that Man was knowing of his place as the cornerstone of creation, lifted above smallness and raised above little things; tearing the veil of deception from off the eyes of the Spirit that it might read what the clouds had writ on heaven's face, and the breeze on the surface of the water; and know the manner of the flower's breathing and the meaning of the songs of the thrush and the nightingale.

* * *

From beyond the wall of the Present, on the stage
  of days to come —
I saw Beauty as the groom and the Spirit his bride
And Life, in its all, the Night of Power.*

* The twenty-seventh night of Ramadan, the Moslem month of fasting, when the first revelation came to Muhammad. It is said that on this night the gates of paradise are open so that any demand made on God or the Prophet will go direct to them.

THE QUEEN OF FANTASY

I came to the ruins of Palmyra and, wearied by
my journey thereto, I cast myself down on the grass
that grew among pillars and columns broken by
time and brought level with the earth. And when
night fell with the gathering together of scattered
creation beneath a cloak of silence, I felt an aware-
ness in the air about me of something that flowed,
fragrant as incense and intoxicating as wine. I drank
of it and felt hidden hands playing with my senses,
and my eyelids grew heavy and my spirit was freed
from its fetters. Then the earth opened and the
firmament trembled and I leaped forward, impelled
thither by an unearthly force. And I found myself
in the midst of a garden whose like no human creature had imagined. About me was a company of
virgins who were clothed in no garment save that
of beauty. They walked around me, and as they
walked, it was as though their feet touched not the
ground. They chanted melodies woven from dreams

of love and played upon lyres wrought of ivory and having strings of gold.

And I came to an opening and beheld in its midst a throne encrusted with precious stones. It was in a meadow from out of which flowed light and divers colors of the rainbow. On the right hand and the left stood the virgins. They lifted up their voices and looked toward a part wherefrom rose the smell of myrrh and frankincense. And lo, there came out from among the flowering branches a Queen, who walked slowly toward the throne and set herself upon it. Then a flight of doves, white as driven snow, descended, and they settled themselves about her feet in the form of a crescent.

The virgins chanted verses in praise of their Queen, and the incense ascended in columns to her glory. The while I stood and looked upon what no other man's eye had seen and heard what no human ear had heard.

Then the Queen made a sign with her hand, and all movement ceased. In a voice that made my spirit tremble as lute strings under the player's fingers, and moved everything in that enchanted place as though the things were ears and hearts, she said:

"I have called you hither, human, for I am the mistress of the regions of fantasy. I have granted you leave to stand before me, for I am Queen over the glade of dreams. Hearken, therefore, to my commands and proclaim them abroad among mankind.

86

Say that the city of fantasy is a wedding feast, and its gate is guarded by a mighty man of valor, and no person may enter therein except he be clad in wedding garments. Say that it is a paradise whose overseer is the angel of Love, and no man may cast eyes thereon save him who has the sign of Love on his brow. It is a field of imaginings whose rivers are as good wine; whose birds cleave the air as angels; whose flowers are prodigious of their fragrance; whose ground none treads save the child of dreams.

"Speak with men and say that I granted them a cup brimful of joy, but they in their folly did pour it out and the angel of darkness came and filled it with a draught of grief. And this did they swallow up and were drunk of it. Say you that none can play upon the stringed instrument of Life save one whose finger tips have touched my girdle and whose eyes have looked upon my throne.

"Isaiah uttered verses of wisdom as a necklace of pearls strung on strands of my love. John related his vision in my tongue. And Dante trod not the pasture of souls except with my guidance. I am a symbol embracing reality; and a truth revealing the oneness of the spirit; a witness testifying to the deeds of the gods. Say: In truth, thought has a resting-place above the world of visible things, whose heaven is not obscured by the clouds of joy. And visions have form in the heaven of the gods and are reflected in the mirror of the soul so that its hope

87

may be in all that is to be after its release from the world of matter."

Then the Queen of Fantasy drew me toward her with a look of enchanting and kissed my burning lips, saying: "Say that who passes not his days in the region of dreams is the slave of those days."

Thereupon the voices of the virgins ascended and the smoke of the incense receded and twisted upwards into the air and the vision departed. A second time the earth opened and the firmament trembled and I beheld myself back among the ruins.

The dawn broke smiling, and on my tongue and between my lips were the words: "Who passes not his days in the region of dreams is the slave of those days."

MY BLAMER

Leave me, my blamer, in my solitude.
By the love that binds your spirit
To the beauty of the loved one,
I adjure you;
By the love that makes one your heart
With a mother's tenderness,
And holds you close to a child's affection,
I pray you, leave me;
Forsake me and my dreams.
I will wait upon the morrow
And it shall judge me as it will.

Advice and counsel you gave me,
But advice is naught save a specter
Beckoning the spirit to confusion's abode
And leading it whither life is cold as earth.

I have a little heart;
I would free it from the darkness of my breast

To bear it in my palm,
Seeking its depths and asking its secrets.
Loose not your shafts at it, my blamer,
Lest you cause it to fear, and hide
Within its cage of ribs
Ere it pour out its secret's blood,
And do what the gods did will it
When they fashioned it of love and beauty.

The sun is risen
And the nightingale is trilling
And the spirit of the myrtle ascends.
I would be free of sleep's covering
To wander with the white lambs.
Frighten me not, my blamer,
With the lion of the forest
And the vipers of the valley,
For my spirit knows not fear
Nor is aware of evil ere its coming.

Leave me, my blamer,
Exhort me not,
For affliction has opened my eyes,
And tears given me sight.
Grief has taught me the language of hearts.

Cease this recital of things forbidden,
For my conscience is a tribunal
That will judge me with justice.

It will guard me from punishment if I am innocent,
And withhold from me favor when I am guilty.

The procession of love goes its way
And beauty walks with manner aloft;
And youth, too, sounding horns of joy.
Do not prevent me, my blamer,
But let me go;
For the way is strewn with roses and fragrant herbs.
And censers of musk have perfumed the air.

Free me from stories of riches and tales of glory,
For my spirit is satisfied
And busied with the glory of the gods.

Absolve me from things of pomp and state,
For the earth in its all is my land,
And all mankind my countrymen.

SOLILOQUY

Where are you, my love,
Are you in that little garden watering the flowers
That love you as infants love their mother's breast?
Or in your little room, wherein you have raised to
    innocence an altar
And sacrificed upon it my spirit and my heart?
Or mayhap amidst your books
Harvesting the wisdom of men —
You who are so rich in the wisdom of the gods?

Where are you, companion of my spirit?
Are you in the sanctuary praying for me?
Or in the meadow calling to Nature —
The haven of your wonder and dreams?
Or mayhap in the houses of the wretched
Consoling those of broken heart
With the sweetness of your self,
And giving of your bounty to fill their hands?

You are in all places, for you are the spirit of God,
And in all times, for you are greater and stronger
    than time itself.

Remember you the nights of our union
And the light of your spirit that was as a halo about
    us?
And the angels of love that hovered above us
Singing and chanting in the things of the spirit?

Remember you the days when we sat beneath the
    boughs
That cast o'er us a covering
And concealed us from the sight of men
As ribs conceal the sacred secrets of the heart?
And the paths and the slopes we trod, our fingers in-
    terwoven,
When we leaned our heads one against the other
As though to take refuge from ourselves within our-
    selves?

Remember you the hour I came to say farewell?
You embraced me and kissed me the kiss of Mary.
And I learned that where the lips embrace
They utter divine secrets the tongue knows not.
A kiss it was, the prelude to a sigh,
As the breath the Almighty breathed into clay —
And made it man.

Thus is the sigh that goes before us to the world of
	spirits,
Proclaiming the glory of our twin souls.
There shall it remain until we and it are joined
For eternity.

Again did you kiss and embrace me,
Saying, with tears flowing from your eyes:
"In truth have earthly bodies desires unbeknown
And must they ofttimes separate for earthly pur-
	pose,
And remain apart for worldly reason.
But all spirits abide in safety in love's hands
Till Death do come and bear them aloft to God.
Go, then, my darling, for Life has made you her
	delegate.
Go, obey her.
She is a comely woman, giving them that obey her
To drink from the limpid Poot * of joy in full.
As for me, your love has given me a waiting groom,
And your memory, an eternal wedding."

Where are you now, my companion?
Are you awake in the still night,
Waiting on a breeze
That shall carry my heartbeats and innermost
	thoughts
Toward you?

* In Arabic, *Kauthar*, River of Paradise.

Or seeing the picture of your young love?
That picture is no more like the pictured,
For sadness has cast its shadow
Upon a face yesterday rejoicing in your presence,
And weeping has withered eyes your beauty did
    anoint.
Grief has parched a mouth moistened by your kisses.

Whither are you, beloved?
Do you hear my call and lament beyond the oceans?
See you my weakliness and abasement —
Know you of my patience and enduring?
Are there not in space spirits
To bear the last breath of a dying one?
Are there not between souls hidden strands
To carry the complaint of a lover in sickness?

Where are you, beloved?
Darkness enfolds me,
And mourning is victor.
Smile into the air and I shall be refreshed;
Breathe into the ether and I shall live.

Where are you, beloved, where . . . ?
Ah, How mighty is love,
How does it diminish me!

THE CRIMINAL

A youth sat on the roadside begging alms; a youth strong of body, made weak by hunger. There he sat with his hands stretched forth, asking of the passers-by, entreating the charitable and bewailing his lot, and crying out against the pangs of hunger.

Night fell; his lips were dry and his tongue heavy and his hands and stomach empty.

Soon he rose and went outside the city and sat him beneath the trees and wept a bitter weeping. He lifted up his tear-filled eyes and his hunger spoke, saying: "O Lord, I went to the wealthy seeking work and they turned me away because of my tattered garments. I knocked on the door of a school and they forbade me entry because my hands were empty. I sought to labor for my daily bread, but people rejected me because my star was against me. So did I come to beg.

"They that adore Thee, O Lord, beheld me and said this one is strong and able; charity is not for him given to sloth and idleness. My mother bore me at Thy willing; now by Thee do I exist. Wherefore do people deny to me the bread that I seek in Thy name?"

And on that very minute the countenance of that despairing man changed. He rose on his feet, and his eyes shone like a bright star. Then from the dried branches he fashioned for himself a stout club. He pointed with it toward the city and shouted: "I sought life with the sweat of my brow and found it not. Now shall I take it with the strength of my forearm. I begged for bread in love's name, but no man heard me. Now shall I seek it in the name of evil. . . ."

Many years passed and that youth severed necks for the sake of their adornment, and destroyed bodies to satisfy his appetite. He increased in riches and was renowned for his strength and violence. He was beloved among the plunderers of the people and feared by the law-abiding. One day the Amir appointed him deputy in that town, in the manner of all princes who chose those to speak in their name.

Thus do men in their greed make of the wretched criminals, and with their harshness drive the child of peace to kill.

THE BELOVED

THE FIRST GLANCE

'Tis the minute separating life's ecstasy from its awakening; and the first light to illumine the vast fields of the spirit.

The first enchanting note upon the first string of the heart's lyre;

The instant that brings back to the ear of the spirit the mention of bygone days, and reveals to its sight the happenings of nights past, and shows to its understanding deeds wrought by joy and grief in this world, and the secret of immortality in the world to come.

'Tis the seed that Astarte casts down from the heights to be sown by the eyes in the field of the heart, and nurtured by love and brought to fruit by the spirit.

The first glance from the beloved is like the Spirit that hovered over the face of the deep, out of which came heaven and earth;

The first glance from the companion of life's way is as the word of God when He said: "Be."

THE FIRST KISS

'Tis the first sip of a cup that the gods have filled from the limpid pool of Love. The dividing line between doubt that saddens the heart and certainty that makes it joyful.

The first line of the poem of unearthly life; the first chapter of the story of man in the spirit.

A link joining the wonder of the past with the future's splendor; uniting the silence of feeling with its song.

A word uttered by four lips making the heart a throne, and love a sovereign, and fulfillment a crown.

A soft touch like the fingertips of the breeze in their passing over the rose, bearing a sigh of gladness and a sweet moaning.

The beginning of disturbance and trembling that separate lovers from the world of matter and transport them to the regions of inspiration and dreams.

And if the first glance is as the seed that the goddess of love sows in the field of the human heart, the first kiss is as the first blossom on the first branch of the tree of life.

UNION

Here, then, does love begin in making life's prose verse, creating from the mysteries of existence chapters chanted by the days and nights.

Thus does longing tear away the veil from the secrets of past years and fashion from the smallest joy happiness transcended only by the soul's bliss when it embraces its Lord.

Union is the fusion of two divinities to create a third on earth; the binding together of two strong in their love against an adversary weak in its hating.

'Tis the casting away by two spirits of discord and their oneness with unity.

The golden link in a chain whose first is a glance, whose last is the Infinite.

The fall of refreshing rains from heaven upon sanctified Nature to distill strength from the blessed fields.

And if the first glance from the eyes of a loved one is as the seed sown by Love in the field of the heart,

Then is the first kiss of her lips as the first blossom on the tree of life.

And in her union is the first fruit of that sowing.

THE ABODE OF HAPPINESS

My heart was weary within me and bade me farewell and repaired to the Abode of Happiness. And
when it was come to that sanctuary which the spirit
had sanctified, it stood in wonderment, for it saw
not there things it had imagined.

It saw not there power or wealth, nor yet authority. It saw naught save the youth of Beauty and
his companion the daughter of Love and their child
Wisdom.

Then my heart spoke to the daughter of Love and
said: "Where is contentment, O Love? I had heard
that it shared with you this dwelling." And she answered: "Contentment is away preaching in the
city, where is corruption and greed; we are not in
need of it in this place. Happiness desires not contentment, for happiness is naught but a longing that
union embraces; contentment is a diversion conquered by forgetfulness. The immortal soul is not

contented, for it is ever desiring of perfection; and perfection is the Infinite."

And my heart spoke to the youth of Beauty and said: "Show to me the secret of woman, O Beauty, and enlighten me, for you are knowledge." He said: "She is you, human heart, and as you were, so was she. She is I, and wheresoever I be, there is she. She is as a religion when the ignorant profane it not; as a full moon when clouds do not hide it; as the breeze untouched by corruption and impurity."

Then my heart drew near to Wisdom, the daughter of Love and Beauty, saying: "Give me wisdom that I may carry it to humankind." She answered: "Say that happiness begins in the holy of holies of the spirit and comes not from without."

THE CITY OF THE PAST

Life stood with me at the foot of the mountain of youth and pointed to what was behind us. I looked, and beheld a city of strange form and pattern in the bosom of the plains, wherein were images and ascending smokes of divers colors. And the whole was veiled in a fine mist, almost obscured from sight.

I said: "What thing is this, Life?"

She answered: "It is the City of the Past. Observe it well."

And I observed and saw places of work sitting like great giants beneath the wings of slumber. And sanctuaries of words around which hovered souls crying out in despair — and singing in hope. I beheld temples of religion set up by faith and destroyed by doubting. And minarets of thoughts rising heavenward like hands uplifted for alms.

Streets of desires flowing like rivers between hills I saw. And storehouses of secrets guarded by silence and plundered by thieves of inquiring. Towers of progress builded by courage and overthrown by fear.

Palaces of dreams that the nights adorned and awakening spoiled. Dwellings of littleness inhabited by weakness; and places of aloneness wherein rose self-denial. Meeting-places of knowledge illumined by wisdom and darkened by folly. Wineshops of love wherein lovers drank, mocked by emptiness.

Stages of life whereon Life plays her piece; to which Death comes to end his tragedy.

That, then, is the City of the Past. A city far off, yet near; seen and unseen.

Then Life walked before me and said: "Follow me, for we have tarried long." And I asked: "Whither now, Life?" She answered: "To the City of the Future." Said I: "Have pity, for the journey has surely wearied me, and my feet have trodden stones, and obstacles have drunk my strength."

"Come, for only the coward tarries, and it is folly to look back on the City of the Past."

MEETING

When the night had completed its adornment of heaven's robe with the stars' jewels, there ascended from the Valley of the Nile a nymph having invisible wings. She sat upon a throne of clouds raised high above the Mediterranean Sea, which was made silver by the moonlight. Before her passed a heavenly host of spirits chanting, "Holy, holy, holy to the daughter of Egypt, whose glory filleth the earth."

And there rose from the mouth of a waterspout in the forest of the cedars the form of a youth borne by the hands of the seraphim, and he sat upon the throne by the side of the nymph. The spirits passed again, before them both, crying: "Holy, holy, holy to the youth of Lebanon, whose glory filleth the ages."

And when the lover took the hand of his beloved and looked into her eyes, the winds and the waves carried the communion of the one with the other to all the corners of the earth.

How perfect is thy splendor, O daughter of Isis, and how great my love for thee!

How comely art thou among the youths, O son of Astarte, and how great my longing for thee!

My love is like unto thy Pyramids, beloved, and the ages shall not destroy it.

My love is as thy Cedars, beloved, and the elements shall not conquer it.

The wise ones of the earth come from East and West to taste of thy wisdom and inquire of thy signs.

And the great ones of the earth come from many lands to drink the wine of thy beauty and the magic of thy mysteries.

In truth, beloved, are thy palms the source of abundance to fill the storehouses.

In truth, beloved, are thine arms the fount of sweet waters, and thy breath a refreshing breeze.

The palaces of the Nile and its temples proclaim thy glory, and Father of Terror * telleth of thy greatness, my love.

The cedars upon thy breast are a mark of nobleness, and the towers about thee chant thy might and valor, my love.

How goodly is thy love and how sweet is the hope of thine exaltation, beloved!

* I.e., the Sphinx.

How generous a companion art thou and how sufficient a spouse! How fine are thy gifts and how precious thine offerings! Thou sendest to me young men and they are as an awakening from deep sleep. Thou givest me a man of valor to overcome my people's feebleness; and a sage to raise them; a noble man to ennoble them.

I have sent to thee seeds and thou hast made them to flower; and young shoots and thou hast raised them as trees. For thou art the virgin field that giveth life to the rose and the lily and bringeth up the cypress tree and the cedar. . . .

SECRETS OF THE HEART

In a fine palace standing in the dark night like Life in the shadow of Death a maiden sat in a chair of ivory. Her head was supported by her hand in the manner of a withered flower leaning upon its petals. She looked about her like a prisoner without hope who would pierce the prison wall with his eyes to look at life ever moving in the procession of freedom.

The hours passed as phantoms in the darkness, what time the maiden solaced herself with tears and took refuge in her solitude and grief. And when the violence of her feeling became heavy on her heart and unlocked the treasury of her secret thoughts, she took up a pen, and her tears flowed with the ink. And she wrote thus:

"Beloved sister: When the heart is straitened with that which it conceals and eyelids are oppressed with tears and ribs are nigh torn asunder with growing hidden things, what is there for man save speech and complaint? The saddened deems complaint a sweet thing, and the lover finds consolation in the fire of his youth, and the oppressed sees relief in supplication. . . . Now do I write to you thus because I am become a poet who beholds the beauty of all things and arranges the pattern of that beauty impelled by the power of his divineness. Or as a starveling child seeing succor, driven by the bitterness of its hunger, unmindful of its mother's poverty and destitution.

"Hearken to my pitiful tale, my sister, and weep for me. For weeping is like prayer, and the tears of compassion are as a good deed that goes not unrequited; they ascend from the depths of the spirit, a living thing. . . . My father joined me in marriage with a man of riches and station, the like of all fathers of possessions and honor who wish to propagate wealth by wealth; fearing poverty and embracing honor with honor as a refuge from the shame of days. And so I and my dreams and longings were sacrificed on an altar of gold that I held as naught; to high estate, which was hateful in my sight. I was a prey trembling in the grasp of matter which, if it be not made to serve the spirit, is harsher than death and bitterer than the grave. I hold in esteem my lord, for he is generous and honorable and strives in the way of my happiness and pursues riches for my delight. But I have found that all these things are not worth one moment of a true

109

and sanctified love; that love which holds as naught all things and remains mighty.

"Do not mock at me, my sister, for I am now become the most knowing of people in the things of a woman's heart, that palpitating heart, that bird fluttering in the firmament of love. That vessel overflowing with the wine of ages prepared for the lips of the soul. That book wherein are writ chapters of joy and grief; happiness and misery; pleasure and pain. That book none shall read save the true companion, the half of woman that is created for her from the beginning to the end of time. . . .

"Ay, I have known women in their longings and desires since I saw that my lord's fine horses and carriages and his ever filled coffers and high estate were not the equal of one glance from the eyes of a poor youth who entered this existence for my sake and for whom I did come. A patient one waiting in grief and the wretchedness of separation. And oppressed one sacrified to my father's will; imprisoned without guilt in the dungeons of time. . . . Seek not to console me, for out of my affliction is a consoler, the knowledge of my love's power and the honor of my yearning and longing. I look now from beyond my tears and behold my lot, day by day, drawing nigh to lead me whither I shall await the companion of my spirit and meet with him and embrace him a long and sacred embrace. Reproach me not, for I do as is proper to a faithful wife, sub-

mitting to the laws and customs of men with forbearance and enduring. I honor my lord and esteem
him and laud him, but I am not able of giving him
my all, for God has already granted that to my beloved ere I knew him. Heaven has willed in its hidden wisdom that I pass my days with a man other
than for whom I was created, and I shall pass this
existence in silence in accordance with Heaven's
willing. And when the doors of eternity are open
and I am joined with the half of my spirit, I shall
look back upon the past — and the past is this very
present — as does the spring on winter. I shall ponder on this life as one who has gained the summit
considers the passes through which he has come ere
attaining it."

Here the maid ceased from writing. She covered
her face with her hands and gave herself to bitter
weeping as though her great spirit rebelled against
the committing to paper of the holiest of her secrets.
She dried her tears quickly and they were gone to
abide in the gentle air, the resting-place of the souls
of lovers and flowers.

After a while she took up again her pen and
wrote:

"Do you remember that youth, my sister? Do
you remember the light shining from his eyes, and
the sadness impressed upon his brow, and his smile
that was like the tears of a bereaved woman? Do
you recall his voice, which was as the echo of a far-

off valley? Do you call him to memory when he would ponder on things with a long silent look, and speak of them in wonder, and incline his head and sigh as though in fear that speech would betray what was concealed in his depths? And his dreams and beliefs, those too do you remember? Ay, these many things in a youth whom other men thought their like, whom my father did despise because he was raised above dross and more honorable than that he should inherit honor from his forebears.

"Ay, my sister, well do you know that I am a martyr of the small things of this world and a sacrifice to folly. Show pity to your sister, who sits up in the silent watches of the night to uncover to you the secrets of her breast. Have compassion, for love did likewise visit your heart."

Morning came and the maiden rose from her writing and soon sleep overtook her. Mayhap she would find therein dreams sweeter than the dreams of awakening.

THE BLIND FORCE

Spring came and Nature spoke in the tongues of brooks and streams and made glad the heart. And she smiled on the lips of flowers and made rejoice the spirit.

Then she waxed wroth and razed the fine city and caused men to forget the sweetness of her words and the tenderness of her smile.

A blind and terrifying force destroying in a minute what the ages had builded. A merciless death clutching at throats with sharpened talons and crushing without ruth. A consuming fire swallowing sustenance and life. A black night concealing the beauty of life beneath a covering of obscurity.

Terrifying elements blowing from their resting-places to do battle with man in his weakness and destroy his dwelling-places, scattered in a second what he has gathered in an hour. A mighty earthquake, which the earth conceived, and in travail bore naught save destruction and despair.

And so it was, the while the grieving spirit looked on from afar, sorrowing and reflecting. It pondered upon the limited night of men before unseen forces, and sorrowed with the fleeing victims of fire and ruin. It reflected on the enmity of man hidden beneath layers of earth and in the very particles of the air.

It sorrowed with the lamenting mothers and the hungry children, and thought on the cruelty of matter and its belittlement of life. It shared likewise the suffering of those that yestereve did sleep in safety in their houses, who today are standing afar, mourning the fine city with broken sobs and bitter tears.

It saw how hope was become despair, and joy sorrow, and rest unrest. And it grieved with hearts trembling in the grasp of sadness and despair and torment.

Thus did stand the spirit betwixt sorrow and reflection. Now led to doubt the justice of those divine laws binding the forces one to the other; now turning back and murmuring into the ears of the stillness:

"In truth is there beyond creation an eternal wisdom born of calamities and scourges that we behold, but whose good fruits we see not. And the fires and earthquakes and tempests are to the earth's body as are hatred and envy and evil in the human heart.

They rage and storm and then are still. And from out of their raging and storming and stillness create the gods a beautiful knowledge, which man purchases with his tears and his blood and gains.

"I stand in remembrance. The tragedy of this people fills the ears with sighing and lamenting. And before my eyes appear the tears and misfortunes that have crossed the stage of the days.

"I have seen man in all his generations set up on the earth's breast towers and palaces and temples, and the earth has taken them back to her heart.

"I have seen likewise the strong build firm buildings, and workers in stone create from the rock pictures and images. And tracers adorn walls and gates with painting and drawing. And I have seen this earth open wide its mouth and swallow up the creation of artful hands and profound minds. Blotting out in its harshness the pictures and images; destroying in its anger the tracings and the drawings; burying in its wrathfulness the noble walls and columns; making fine dwellings bare of the adornments with which men had adorned them; putting in the stead of the meadow's green garment stuff embroidered with gold of the sand and the jewelry of stones and pebbles."

Yet did I find among these wrongs and misfortunes the divinity of man standing upright as a giant mocking at earth's foolishness and the anger of the elements. And like a pillar of light standing out of the ruins of Babylon and Nineveh and Palmyra, and Bombay and San Francisco, it sang a hymn of immortality, saying: "Let the earth then take what is to it; for I am without end."

TWO WISHES

In the stillness of the night Death descended from God on the sleeping city and abode upon the highest tower therein. He pierced the walls of the houses with his brilliant eyes and saw in them spirits borne away on the wings of dreams, and bodies given up to slumber.

And when the moon waned at the approach of dawn and the city was covered with an enchanted veil, Death walked with soft footsteps among those dwellings until he reached the mansion of the rich man. He entered therein and there was none to stop him. He stood by the bedside and touched the eyelids of the sleeper. The rich man woke in terror. And when he saw the specter of Death before him, he cried out in a voice in which were fear and rage:

"Get you from me, terrible dream! Go, evil spirit! How did you enter, thief, and what do you want, snatcher? Go, then, for I am master of this house.

Away with you, lest I call the slaves and the guards to tear you to pieces!"

Then Death drew near and in a voice of thunder roared: "I am Death; therefore take heed and be humble."

And the rich and powerful man asked: "What want you from me now, and what thing do you seek? Why have you come whilst yet my work is unfinished? What do you wish from the powerful like me? Go you to the sickly. Get you hence from me and show me not your whetted talons and hair that hangs like coiling snakes. Go, for the sight of your terrible wings and corrupt body is hateful to me." But after an uneasy silence he spoke again and said:

"No, no, kind Death, take no heed of what I said, for fear makes me speak words my heart would forbid. Take, then, a measure of my gold or the soul of one of my slaves and leave me. . . . I have account with life yet unfulfilled and wealth with people not yet gathered. I have on the seas ships not yet come to port, and in the earth produce not yet garnered. Take you of these things what you will and leave me. Concubines I have, fair as the morning, for your choosing, Death. Hearken further: I have an only son whom I love, the apple of my eye. Take him too, but leave me alone."

Then Death put his hand on the mouth of this

slave of earthly life and took his reality and gave it up to the air.

Death proceeded on his way through the quarters of the poor until he reached a humble dwelling. He entered therein and approached a bed on which lay a young man. After gazing on his tranquil countenance he touched his eyes and the youth awoke. And when he saw Death standing above him he fell upon his knees and lifted his hands toward him and in a voice touched by the spirit's longing and love, said:

"Here I am, beautiful Death. Receive my spirit, reality of my dreams and substance of my hopes. Embrace me, beloved of my soul, for you are merciful and will not abandon me here. You are the messenger of the gods. You are the right hand of truth. Leave me not. How long have I sought you without finding, and called upon you and you hearkened not! But now have you heard me, therefore do not meet my love with shunning. Embrace my soul, my beloved Death."

Then Death put his gentle fingers upon the boy's lips and took his reality and put it beneath his wings.

And when Death cleft the air, he looked back at this world, and into the void blew these words:

"Who has not come from the Infinite shall not return to the Infinite."

THE PLAYGROUND OF LIFE

A minute moving among the patterns of Beauty
and the dreams of Love is greater and more precious than an age filled with splendor granted by the
weak to the strong.

From that minute rises the god-state of man, and
in that age it sleeps a deep sleep veiled by a veil of
disturbing dreams;

In that minute is the spirit freed from the bur-
dens of men's conflicting laws,

And in that age is it prisoned behind walls of
neglect and weighted with chains of oppression.

That minute was the cradle of Solomon's song
and the Sermon on the Mount and the lyrics of al-
Farid. That age was blind force that destroyed the
temples of Baalbek and razed the palaces of Palmyra and Babylon's towers.

A day spent by the soul in lamenting the death of
the rights of the poor man and in weeping for the

loss of justice is nobler than the age lost by a man in enjoyment of his appetite.

That day purifies the heart with its fire and fills it with its light; and that age envelops it with its dark wings and buries it 'neath layers of earth.

That day was the day of Sinai and of Calvary and the Flight.* That age did Nero pass in the market place of wrongs, and Korah set it up on the altar of lust, and Don Juan buried it in the grave of bodily desires.

And so is life. Played by the nights on the stage of destiny as a tragedy; sung by the days as a hymn. And in the end guarded by Eternity as a jewel.

* The flight, or Hegira, of Muhammad to Medina.

MY FRIEND

If you knew, my poor friend, that the poverty
which condemns you to misery is that same thing
which inspires in you the knowledge of justice and
gives you understanding of life's meaning, you
would be satisfied with God's ruling.

You would say: The knowledge of justice; for
the rich man is buried in his treasury away from
that knowledge. Life's meaning; for the powerful
leave it aside in their pursuit of glory.

Rejoice, then, in justice, for you are its mouth-
piece; and in life, for you are its book. Be glad, for
you are the source of the merit of those who help
you and the strong arm of the virtue of them that
take your hand.

If you knew, my sad friend, that the misfortune
that has overtaken you is the force that illumines
the heart and raises up the spirit from mocking to
esteem, you would be content with it for a heritage

and praise it for a guidance. And from it you would know that life is a chain, its links taking hold one of another. And that grief is a golden link separating submission to the present from business with future's joy, as morning comes between sleep and awakening.

In truth, my friend, poverty manifests nobleness of spirit, and riches reveal its littleness.

Grief softens our feeling, and rejoicing hardens. For men have not ceased to use wealth and joy as a means to increasing, even as they do in the name of the Book evil of which the Book is innocent. And in the name of humanity that which humanity rejects.

Were poverty to be banished and grieving be no more, then were the spirit a page empty save of symbols showing selffulness and amassing, and words telling of earthly lusts.

For I have looked and have found a divineness, the unearthly self in man, that is not sold for riches or developed by the joys of the time. I have considered, and I have seen the rich man cast aside his godlikeness to covet his riches; and the young men of the age forsake it in pursuit of their pleasures.

The hour, my friend, that you pass with the companion of your days and your little ones on your return home from the fields is a symbol of the human family in ages to come: it is the sign of the happiness of future days. And the life that the rich man passes in the counting-house is in truth an existence likened to the existence of worms in the grave: the symbol of fear.

And the tears you shed, my grieving one, they are sweeter than the laughing of one seeking to forget, and pleasanter than loud voices in jest. Those tears shall cleanse the heart of hating and teach him that sheds them to be companion to those of broken heart. They are the tears of the Nazarene.

The strength you sow, poor one, which is reaped by the powerful, shall return to you, for all things return to their source in Nature's dispensation.

The grief you have borne shall be turned into gladness on Heaven's command. And coming ages shall learn equality from poverty, and love through grieving.

A TALE OF LOVE

In a lonely house sat a youth in the morning of his life. He sat looking now through the window at the starry sky, now at the picture of a woman in his hand. A picture it was the line and color of which were reflected in his face. The picture of a woman's face speaking to him and making his eyes ears; putting in him understanding of the language of the hovering spirits in that room; bringing to birth hearts lighted by love and filling with yearning.

So passed the hour as a minute of pleasant dreaming, or as a year from eternity. Then the youth set the picture before him and took up pen and paper and wrote:

"Beloved of my soul: Great and sublime truths pass not from one human creature to another by way of human speech; rather do they choose silence as a road between souls. I know that the stillness of this night is a messenger between our two spirits bearing messages even more tender than those the breeze writes upon the water's face; reciting the pages of our two hearts to each other. As God willed that our souls be placed in the prison of our bodies, so did love decree that I should be the prisoner of words.

"They say, my darling, that love through worship turns into an all-consuming fire. I have found that the hour of separation does not prevail against the joining of our unearthly selves, as I have known with the first meeting that my spirit was your companion for countless ages, and that your first glance was not, in truth, the first glance.

"Ah, my love, verily the hour that did join our two hearts exiled from another world was one among many that upheld my believing in the eternity of the spirit and its immortality. In such an hour does Nature tear away the veil from the face of timeless justice that people think injustice.

"Do you recall, beloved, the garden wherein we stood, each regarding the face of a loved one? And your glances told me your love for me sprang not from pity. Those glances taught me to proclaim to myself and to the world that the gift whose source is justice is greater than that which begins in charity. And love that is created of circumstance is like the waters of a swamp.

"Before me, my love, is a life I would to be great and beautiful. A life that will be dear to the memory of future men and evoke their love and esteem. A life whose beginning was your meeting, of whose immortality I was assured. For I believed that your being was able to bring back the strength that God had taken from me. Yea, even as the sun brings forth fragrant flowers of the field. And so does my love remain to me and to the ages and endure free from selffulness, that it may be spread abroad and be raised above small things in its devotion to you."

The youth rose and walked across the room slowly. Then he looked again from the window and saw that the moon was risen, filling the firmament with its gentle radiance. He returned to the letter and wrote:

"Forgive me, beloved, for I have spoken to you as another person, yet you are my half that I lost when we emerged from the hand of God on the same moment. Forgive me."

THE DUMB BEAST

*"In the glance of a dumb beast is speech
understood by the souls of the wise."*

AN INDIAN POET

One evening when images took possession of my
mind, I passed by the outskirts of the town and
stood before a deserted house. Its walls were crumbling and its supports falling, and there remained
of it naught save traces to show of its long abandonment and decay.

Then I perceived a dog lying down in the dust,
his weak body overrun with sores and his meager
form emaciated by sickness. He was looking toward
the setting sun with eyes veiled by the shadows of
misery and despair. It was as though he knew that
the sun was withdrawing its warm breath from that
deserted place, far from the children who persecuted
the helpless beast. He gazed at the setting sun with
sorrow and a parting.

I drew near to him slowly, wishing that I knew
his speech that I might console him in the extremity
of his grief and show to him compassion in his de-

spair. At my approach he took fright and moved with what remained to him of a life nearing its end, and sought escape with limbs withered by illness and watched by corruption. And since he was no more able to rise, he looked at me a look in which were the bitterness of imploring and the sweetness of supplication; a look in which were affection and reproach. A look that took the place of speech; which was clearer than the words of men and more eloquent than a woman's tears. When my eyes met his sad ones my feelings moved me and my emotions bestirred themselves, and his glances took body and became voiced speech customary among mankind. And this is what they said:

"Enough, such and such a one. Sufficient that which I have borne of men's cruelty and suffered of pain and ill. Pass you by and leave me and my silence. I shall ask succor of the warming rays of the sun. I have fled from the harshness and oppression of man and sought refuge in the dust, which is softer than his heart, and concealed myself in ruins less desolate than his soul. Get you hence, for what are you if not of the dwellers of an earth bereft of all justice? I am a lowly animal, but I have served the son of man. I have been to him an ever faithful companion and a comfort in his house. In his sorrow I was partner, and his joy was my joy. I remembered him in times of absence and welcomed him on his homecoming. I was satisfied when he threw me the scraps from his table and was happy with a bone his teeth had gnawed clean. But when I grew old and infirm with age, and illness took me, he cast me forth from his house and made me the plaything of cruel boys of the streets and a target for the slings and arrows of dirt and disease.

"I, human being, am a helpless animal, but I find a like thing between me and many of your brothers in kind when they are no longer strong enough to gain their sustenance. I am like the soldiers who fight for their land in their youth and make the earth fruitful in middle age, and when the winter of their lives draws near and their value is diminished, they are cast aside and forgotten. I am like a woman who was a lovely maiden that made rejoice the heart of youth and passed the nights as a wife to rear children and bring to being men of the future. A woman who in her old age is despised and forgotten. . . . How cruel you are, human, and how harsh!"

So did speak the glances of that beast. My heart understood whilst my spirit wavered between pity for him and thinking on the children of my kind. And when he closed his eyes I wished not to disturb him, so I went from that place.

PEACE

The storm abated after having compelled all growing things to bend before it. Stars appeared in their semblance of shattered remnants of the lightning upon the sky's face. And the fields were still as though the battle of the elements had never been.

In that hour a maid entered her room and threw herself upon her couch and wept in bitterness. Her sobbing rose and her broken breaths became words.

"Bring him back to me, O Lord, for my tears are dried up and my bowels are turned to water. Return him to me, O Spirit that judgeth with a wisdom transcending men's prudence, for my spirit fails me and grief takes hold of me. Save him from the whetted fangs of war; deliver him from the hands of death and have pity on a frail youth wronged by the power of the strong and snatched from me.

"Conquer, O Love, and vanquish war, your en-

131

emy. Save my loved one, for he is of your sons. Get you hence, O Death, that he may see me, or come you and lead me to him."

On that very moment entered a youth whose head was swathed in white wrappings upon which battle had writ in crimson letters. He came near to the maiden and greeted her with a tear and a smile. Then he took her hand and put it against his lips, and in a voice in which were a wounding love and a joyous meeting said: "Have not fear, for he for whom you weep is come back. Rejoice, then, for peace has restored to you him whom war did take, and magnanimity has returned that which greed did plunder. Dry your tears, my loved one, and smile. Be not astonished at my return alive, for love has a sign before which death flees on beholding; the adversary perceives it and is confused.

"Yea, I am he. Do not think me a phantom come from the regions of darkness to visit a place wherein dwell your beauty and peace. Be not afraid, for I am a truth delivered from fire and sword to bear witness before all people to the victory of love over war. I am a word uttered by a man of peace as a foreword to the tale of your bliss."

With this utterance his tongue became tied and tears took the place of speech. Spirits of rejoicing filled that mean dwelling, and two hearts found that which was lost at their parting.

132

And when morning came, the two stood in a field and looked upon nature's beauty. After a silence in which was converse, the soldier looked toward the east and said to his beloved: "Behold the sun rising from out of darkness."

THE POET

A link
Between this world and the hereafter;
A pool of sweet water for the thirsty;
A tree planted
On the banks of the river of beauty,
Bearing ripe fruits for hungry hearts to seek.

A singing bird
Hopping along the branches of speech,
Trilling melodies to fill all bodies with sweetness
    and tenderness.
A white cloud in the sky at even,
Rising and expanding to fill the heavens,
And then pour out its bounty upon the flowers of
    the fields of Life.

An angel
Sent by the gods to teach man the ways of gods.
A shining light unconquered by the dark,

134

Unhidden by the bushel
Astarte did fill with oil;
And lighted by Apollo.

Alone,
He is clothed in simplicity
And nourished by tenderness;
He sits in Nature's lap learning to create,
And is awake in the stillness of night
In wait of the spirit's descent.
A husbandman who sows the seeds of his heart in
    the garden of feeling,
Where they bring forth yield
To sustain those that garner.

This is the Poet that is unheeded of men in his days,
And is known by them on his quitting the world to
    return to his heavenly abode.
This is he who seeks no thing of men save a little
    smile;
Whose breath rises and fills the firmament with liv-
    ing visions of beauty.
Yet do the people withhold from him sustenance
    and refuge.

Until when, O Man,
Until when, O Existence,
Will you build houses of honor
To them that knead the earth with blood

And shun those who give you peace and repose?
Until when will you exalt killing
And those who make bend the neck beneath the
yoke of oppression?
And forget them that pour into the blackness of
night
The light of their eyes to show you the day's splen-
dor?
Those whose lives are passed in misery
That happiness and delight might not pass you by.

And you, O Poets,
Life of this life:
You have conquered the ages
Despite their tyranny,
And gained for you a laurel crown
In the face of delusion's thorns.
You are sovereign over hearts,
And your kingdom is without end.

MY BIRTHDAY

Written in Paris, 6 December 1908

On this day my mother bore me.

On this day five and twenty years ago the silence put me between the hands of this existence, full with cries and battle and contending.

Thus have I walked round the sun twenty and five times. And I know not how many times the moon has encircled me. Yet I have not unveiled the secrets of life, neither have I known the hidden things of darkness.

I have walked five and twenty times with the earth and the moon and the sun and the planets around the Universal Law.

Behold now my spirit murmuring the names of that Law like caves echoing the voice of sea waves. Its being is in His being, but knows not His essence; it sings the songs of His ebb and flow, but comprehends Him not.

Twenty and five years ago the hand of time wrote me as a word in the book of this strange terrifying world. Behold me, then, a word vague and confused of meaning; now signifying no thing; now meaning many things.

On this day of the year thoughts and reflections and remembrance jostle one the other in my soul. They stand before me as processions of days gone by and show me phantoms of nights long departed. Then they are dispersed as the winds disperse straying clouds at twilight. They dwindle and become faint in the corners of my room like the songs of streams in far-off and empty valleys.

On this day every year come the spirits that have molded my spirit, hastening toward me from all corners of the earth, encircling me with songs of sad remembrance.

Then gently they withdraw and hide behind visible things. They are like birds that descend upon an abandoned threshing-floor and, finding there no grain, flutter awhile ere flying off to another place.

On this day the meaning of my past life rises up before me as a faded mirror into which I look long and see therein naught except the pallid faces of the years like the faces of the dead; and the wrinkled features of hopes and dreams and passions like the features of old men.

Then I close my eyes and look a second time in the mirror and I see naught but my face;

And I look into my face and behold therein a sadness. I examine this sadness and find it dumb and

giving not utterance. Yet could this sadness speak,
it were sweeter than joy.

Much have I loved in these five and twenty years.
And much that I have loved is hateful to people;
and much that I have hated is by them admired.
What I have loved as a boy I cease not now to love.
And that which I now love I shall love to the end
of my days. For love is the all I can attain, and no
person shall deprive me thereof.

Many are the times I have loved death, and called
it by sweet names and wooed it in secret and public
places. Life also have I loved. For death and life are
one to me in beauty, and equal in delight, and part-
ners in the growth of my longing and yearning.
They have shared alike my love and affection.

I have loved freedom, and my love has grown
with the growth of my knowledge of the bondage of
people to falsehood and deceit. And it has spread
with my understanding of their submission to idols
created by dark ages and raised up by folly and pol-
ished by the touch of adoring lips.

But I have loved also those adorers with my un-
fettered love. Yea, I have had pity on them, for they
are blind and kiss the bloody lips of a wild beast
and see not; and suck up the venom of the viper and
feel not. They dig their own graves with their finger-
nails and know not.

I have loved freedom because I have found it to

be a maiden whom aloneness has made sickly and solitude rendered weak until she is become a phantom passing among houses, standing in the streets and calling on the passer-by, who hears not nor heeds her.

In five and twenty years have I loved happiness as have all men. I have awakened each morning and sought it even as they have sought. But I have found it not in their way; neither have I seen its footprints on the sand outside their mansions; nor have I heard echo of its voice coming from within their temples.

But when I sought it in solitude, I heard my spirit thus whisper in my ear, saying: "Happiness is a child born and brought to life in the heart's depths; it comes not to it from without."

And when I opened my heart to see happiness, I found therein its mirror and its couch and garments. It I did not find.

I have loved all people — much have I loved them. In my sight people are of three kinds. One curses life; one blesses it; one observes it. I have loved the first for his despair; the second for his tolerance; the third for his understanding.

Thus have passed twenty and five years. So have gone my days and my nights, hastening on, one on the heels of another; falling from my life as leaves from a tree in the path of autumn winds.

And today, today I stand in remembrance as a

tired wayfarer who stands midway on the ascending road, and I look on this side and that and see not in the past of my life any thing to which I can point before the sun and say: This is to me.

Neither do I find in the seasons of my years any harvest save leaves tinted with drops of ink, and strange scattered tracings full with line and color, harmonious and discordant.

In these dispersed pages and drawings I have buried and interred my feelings and my thoughts and dreams as does the husbandman seeds in the earth.

But the peasant who goes out to the field and sows his seeds in the soil returns with hope to his house at eventide and awaits the season of harvesting and gathering. Not so I. For I have cast forth seeds of my heart and there is no hope, neither is there awaiting.

And now that I am come to this stage of my journey and see the past from beyond a mist of sighing and grieving, and the future from behind the veil of the past, I stand and gaze on existence from my window.

I behold the faces of people and hear their voices rising upwards. I hear the fall of their footsteps among the dwellings and feel the touch of their spirits and the waves of their desires and the beating of their hearts.

I see children at play running and jumping and throwing bits of soil at one another, the while laughing with glee.

And the young men I see walking with firm step, their heads held high as though they would read a poem of youth writ on the margin of clouds lined with sun rays. And the maidens who walk and sway like young boughs and smile like flowers, the while they gaze upon the young men from under lids that flutter with love and desire.

I see old men walking slowly with bent backs, leaning on sticks and looking on the ground, as though seeking between the cracks precious stones they have lost.

So do I stand at my window and look and ponder on these images and shadows in their silent progress through the streets and byways of the city.

Then I look to that which is beyond the city and see the wild parts in their awful beauty and voiced silence, and rising hills and sloping valleys. The erect trees and gently swaying grass and fragrant flowers; the chanting rivers and singing birds.

I look to that which is beyond the wild places and I behold the sea and the wonders and marvels of its depths, its secrets and buried things. Its foaming waves in their anger and scorn; its spume and spray; its rise and its fall. All this do I see.

And I look then to that which is beyond the sea,

and I perceive the limitless firmament with its worlds floating in space, and the brilliant stars and the suns and the moons. And the planets and the fixed stars, and all the contending and reconciled forces of attraction and repulsion do I see, created and borne by that Will, timeless and without limit. Submitting to a Universal Law whose beginning has no beginning and whose end is without end.

Through my window I look and ponder on these things and I am forgetful of the five and twenty years and the ages that preceded them and the centuries that will follow. And my being and my existence are manifest before me, the concealed and the revealed, as the ghost of a child's sigh trembling in the eternal depths of space and its everlasting heights and endless boundaries. And I feel the existence of this ghost, this spirit, this essence, this self I call "I." I feel its stirrings and hear its clamor. Now does it lift its wings upwards and stretch forth its hands in all directions, and sway trembling on this the day which showed it to existence. Now in a voice rising from its holy of holies does it cry:

"Peace, O Life. Peace, O awakening. Peace, O vision.

"Greeting, O day, whose light conquers the earth's darkness. Greeting, O night, whose darkness reveals the light of the firmament.

"Greeting to spring, which renews the earth's youth; to summer, which proclaims the sun's splendor. Greeting to autumn, the giver of labor's fruits and toil's reward; to winter, which brings back in its tempests nature's strength.

"To the years which reveal that which the years have hidden. To the ages which have redressed the wrongs of ages: greeting.

"Peace, O time, who carry us onward to perfection. And peace to you, guiding spirit, who are the reigns of existence; who are hidden from us behind the sun's veil.

"Peace and greeting to you, O heart, because you meditate whilst yet overcome with weeping.

"And to you, O lips, greeting and peace, for verily do you speak peace whilst yet tasting of bitterness."

THE CHILD JESUS

I was alone yesterday in this world, beloved; and my aloneness was as pitiless as death. I was alone as a flower growing in the shadow of mighty rocks, and Life heeded not my existence. And I heeded not the existence of Life.

Today my spirit is awakened and beholds you standing beside it, and its countenance is bright. It prostrates before you even as did the shepherd when he beheld the burning bush.

Yesterday the air's touch was hard and the sun's rays weakly. Mist concealed the earth's face, and the roar of sea waves was like to a howling tempest.

This way I looked and that, and saw not save my self in pain standing beside me. And the shadows of darkness rising and falling about me like hungry ravens.

Today the air is serene and all nature is bathed in light, and the sea waves are at peace and the clouds dispersed. Wheresoever I look do I behold you and see the secrets of life about you like the shimmering spray thrown up by a bird bathing on the lake's placid face.

Yestereve I was a voiceless word in the mind of the night. Today I am become a joyful song on the tongue of the days. And this did come to pass in a minute of time formed of a glance and a word, and a sigh and a kiss.

That minute, my beloved, did join my spirit's past with its future. It was as a white rose rising from the heart of the dark earth to the light of day.

That minute was to my life as was the birth of Jesus to the ages, for it was full with the spirit and purity and love. It made the darkness in my depths as light, and sorrow and despair as good fortune.

The fires of love fall from heaven in divers shapes and forms but they are one in their mark upon the earth.

The little flame that illumines the corners of one man's heart is as the great bright flame that descends from above to light the darkness of nations. For in the one soul are elements and desires and feelings that differ no whit from those within the soul of all mankind.

The Children of Judah, my beloved, awaited the promised coming of a Mighty One since the beginning of time to deliver them from the bondage of the nations.

The great spirit in Greece saw that the worship of Jupiter and Minerva was of no account; and no more was the spirit satisfied.

And in Rome sublime thought considered, and found that the divineness of Apollo was become far from human feeling. And the timeless beauty of Venus was near to old age.

The nations knew, without understanding of the cause thereof, a hunger of the spirit for instruction in affairs transcending matter. And they yearned for a freedom that is not of the body to teach man to rejoice with his neighbor in the light of the sun and the beauty of life.

For, in truth, it is that freedom which draws a man near to the unseen Force without fear or trembling.

All that did come to pass two thousand years before when the yearnings of the human heart were fluttering among visible things, fearing to come near the Immortal, the Universal Spirit. When Pan, god of the forests, was filling with dread the souls of shepherds, and Baal of the sun oppressing the breasts of the lowly and wretched with his priests.

And upon one night, nay, an hour, an instant separated from the ages — for it was stronger than

147

the ages — the lips of the Spirit were opened and they sent forth the Word of Life, which was in the beginning with the Spirit.

And it descended with the light of the stars and the rays of the moon and took form and was a child in the arms of a woman. And it was in a humble place where shepherds guarded their flocks from the perils of the night.

It was a child that slept upon dry straw in a manger;

A sovereign who sat upon a throne fashioned of hearts heavy with the weight of bondage; and souls hungry for the Spirit; and thoughts thirsting for Wisdom.

A suckling child it was, swaddled in his mother's garments, who wrested with his gentleness the scepter of power from the hands of Jupiter and delivered it unto the poor shepherd resting on the earth with his flock.

He it was who took wisdom from Minerva and put it on the tongue of the lowly fisherman sitting in his craft by the shores of the lake.

Who distilled joy through his own sorrow from Apollo and granted it to the brokenhearted standing in entreaty before the door. And poured forth beauty through his beauty from Venus and planted it in the soul of the fallen woman who was afraid of her oppressors.

He it was who brought Baal low from his seat of

power and put in his stead the poor husbandman who sowed seeds in the field by the sweat of his brow.

Was not my suffering, beloved, the suffering of the tribes of Israel of yesteryear?

Did I not watch in the stillness of night for the coming of a Saviour to deliver me from the thrall of days?

Did I not know with the nations in days of yore that deep hunger of the spirit?

Did I not walk on the road of life as a child lost in strange places? And was not my soul as a seed cast onto a stone, which the birds took not up nor destroyed, and the elements cleft not nor brought to life?

All this did come to pass when my dreams sought a dark corner and feared to come near the light.

And upon a night, nay, an hour, an instant discarded from the years of my life, for it was fairer than all the years of my life, the Spirit descended upon me from the circle of light on high and looked upon me with your eyes, and spoke to me with your tongue. From that look and that word sprang love, and it found rest in my broken heart.

A mighty love it was, seated in the manger within my breast; a beautiful love swaddled in clothes of kindness. A gentle suckling lying upon the breast of the spirit, turning my grief into joy and my wretchedness to glory, and making my aloneness a pleasant thing.

A king raised high on the throne of unearthly essence, who brought back with his voice life to my dead days, and light to my weeping eyes with his touch; whose right hand snatched hope from the pit of despair.

The night has been long, my beloved, and now dawn is nigh; soon shall it be day. For the breath of the Child Jesus has filled the firmament and is merged with the air.

My life was a tale of woe; now it is become a joyful thing. And it will be turned to bliss, for the arms of the Child have enfolded my heart and embraced my soul.

COMMUNION OF SPIRITS

Awake, my love, awake!
For my soul calls to you from beyond the raging
    seas;
My spirit stretches forth her wings above the angry
    foaming waves.

Awake, for all is still,
The beat of horse's hoof and the step of passer-by
Are quieted;
And sleep enfolds the souls of men.
But I alone remain awake,
For longing holds me when slumber would engulf
    me,
And love draws me nigh to you
When visions would plant me far.

I have left my couch, beloved,
For I fear the shades of comfort concealed beneath
    the coverings.

I have cast aside the book,
For my sighs erased the lines upon its pages
So that they are white and empty before me.

Awake, awake, beloved, and hearken to me.

Behold me here, my love,
For I have heard your call across oceans
And felt the touch of your wings.
I have left my bed to walk upon the grass,
And the night dew has wetted my feet and my gar-
    ment's hem.
Behold me standing before you 'neath the flower'd
    almond boughs
Hearkening to your call.

Speak then, my beloved,
And let your breath ride with the breeze that comes
    to me from the valleys of Lebanon.
Speak, and none save me shall hear your words,
For night has banished all creation to its rest,
And the dwellers in the city are drunk of sleep.
Alone am I in my wakefulness.

The heavens have woven a veil from moonbeams
And cast it o'er Lebanon's form.
The heavens have fashioned a cloak from the dark-
    ness of night

And lined it with the smoke of workshops and the
breath of Death.
They have concealed within its folds the city's
bones.

Those of the village are aslumber in their huts
Midst the willow and the walnut tree;
And their spirits make haste toward the land of
dreams, my love.

Men are bowed down by the weight of gold,
And greed makes weak their knees.
Their eyes are heavy with trouble and fret,
And they are cast down upon their beds.
Tortured are their hearts, beloved, by specters of
misery and despair.

The phantoms of past ages walk in the valleys,
On the heights the spirits of kings and prophets
wander.
My thoughts have turned toward the places of remembrance
And shown to me the might of Chaldea and the As-
syrian's pride and Arabia's nobility.

In the narrow ways walk the dark ghosts of robbers
And in the crevices of walls vipers of lust rear their
heads;
On street corners the breath of the sickly mingles
with the pangs of death.

Memory has torn aside the curtains of forgetfulness
And revealed to me the abominations of Sodom and
  Gomorrah.

The boughs are swaying, my love,
And the rustling of their leaves
Merges with the murmur of the brook in the valley,
Bringing to our ears
Solomon's song, and the strains of David's lyre,
With the melodies Mausili * made.
The souls of children in the quarter tremble,
And hunger gnaws them.
Their mothers lie in anguish on their beds of misery
  and care,
And dreams of want make the hearts of idle men
  afraid.
I hear deep lament and bitter sighing
That fill the very bones with weeping and mourn-
  ing.

The fragrance of lily and narcissus
Rises and kisses the jasmine's perfume,
And mingles with the sweet breath of cedar
Riding on the breeze above hillocks and winding
  paths;
Filling with love the spirit
And granting it longing
To take the air in flight.

* Ishak al-Mausili (A.D. 767–850), celebrated Arabian musician.

Foul odors from the narrow ways arise,
Mixing with sickness and disease,
And like hidden arrows sharpened, wound
The senses, and the good air fill with poison.

The morning is come, beloved,
And fingers of wakefulness caress
The eyes of them that slumber.
The violet rays are rising from beyond the hills
To toss aside the covering of night
From off Life's splendor and power.
The villages resting in stillness and peace upon the
    shoulders of the valley
Are awakened.
Church bells ring out their praises,
And fill the air with pleasing sounds
Telling that the hour of prayer is nigh.
The caves throw back their chimes in echo
As though all Nature stood in prayer.

The calves have left their stalls,
And the sheep and goats their pens;
They are gone to the meadows to pasture
And eat of the dew-laden glistening grass.
Before them shepherds walk, playing on their pipes,
And behind them the maidens, greeting with the
    birds morning's coming.

The morning is come, beloved,
And upon the crowded dwellings

Day's heavy hand is laid.
Curtains are drawn back from windows,
And doors thrown open.
Tired eyes and troubled faces are revealed
And despairing souls betake themselves to toil.
Within their bodies Death dwells side by side with
      Life;
And the shadows of fear and misery stand astride
      their tightened features
As though they are driven to the shambles.

Behold the streets groaning with the press of hurry-
      ing covetous souls;
The air filled with clank of iron, the grinding of
      wheels, and whistle of steam.
The city is become a battlefield wherein the strong
      contend with the weak,
And the wealthy harvest the labor of the poor.

*   *   *

How beautiful is life, beloved!
'Tis like the heart of a poet,
Full with light and spirit.
How harsh is life, beloved!
'Tis like an evildoer's heart,
Full with guilt and fear.

O WIND

Now singing and rejoicing, now weeping and lamenting.

We hear, but behold you not; we feel your presence yet do not see you.

You were as a sea of love submerging our spirits, yet not drowning us; playing with our hearts in their stillness.

You ascend with the heights and descend with the valleys and are spread out upon fields and meadows.

In your ascending is there strength, and in your descending grace.

You were as a merciful ruler dealing justly with the weak and lowly and showing pride with the strong and mighty.

In autumn do you sigh in the valleys, and the trees weep with you, sighing;

In winter you do shout and roar, and all nature shouts with you.

In spring are you weak and sickly, and in your weakness the fields awake;

In summer you are shrouded in stillness and we take you for dead, slain by the sun's shafts and interred in its heat.

Were you mayhap lamenting in autumn's days, or laughing at the shame of the trees when you rendered them naked?

Were you angry in the days of winter, or dancing about the snow-covered graves of the night?

And in spring were you sickly, or were you a loved one sickened by absence, and come with sighing breath upon the beloved's cheek, the youth of the seasons, to rouse him from his slumber?

Were you perchance dead those summer days, or sleeping in the hearts of fruits, or among the vines or on the threshing-floor?

You bear the breath of illness from city streets, and from the heights the spirit of a flower;

Thus do the great spirits that carry life's agony in silence; and in silence shall we meet its joys.

You murmur wondrous secrets in the ear of the rose, and she understands. Ofttimes she is troubled; ofttimes she smiles. In like manner do the gods with the souls of men.

Here do you tarry; there do you hasten. Thither

you run, but you abide not. So does a man's thought;
it lives by movement and in repose dies.

On the water's face you inscribe verses — then
erase them. Likewise do poets who recite.

From the south you come hot as love.
From the north cold as death;
From the east gentle as the caress of spirits.
From the west you come forth with violence as one
hating.
Are you fickle as the ages, or are you an apostle
come to give us of your faith?

You pass in anger across deserts and trample underfoot the caravans and bury them in graves of
sand.

Are you that hidden flood flowing with the light
of dawn through the leaves of trees?

Passing on like a dream in the valley, where flowers incline for love of you and the plants sway in
ecstasy?

You fall upon the seas in assault and disturb the
peace of their depths so that they rise against you in
anger and open wide their mouths to swallow vessels and souls.

Are you, then, that gentle lover who plays with
the locks of children running among the houses?

Whither are you hastening with our souls and our
spirits and our sighs?

Whither do you carry the pattern of our smiles? What do you with the flaming brands of our hearts in flight?

Do you go with them to where is beyond the twilight — beyond this life? Or drag them as prey to distant caves to blow them hither and thither till they grow faint and die?

In the stillness of night hearts reveal to you their secrets, and with the breaking of dawn the fluttering of lids darkens the eyes.

Are you mindful of what the hearts felt and what the eyes saw?

Between your wings is stored the cry of anguish from the poor man, and the orphan's cry and the mourning woman's lament.

In the folds of your garment the stranger puts his longing, and the forsaken his grief and the fallen woman the cry of her spirit.

Are you the keeper of these lowly ones' trust? Or are you as this earth that takes no thing except to put it to her own body?

Do you hear this cry and this clamor and this weeping? Or are you as the mighty among mankind who heed not the outstretched hand nor hear the voices rising to them?

THE LOVER'S RETURN

Night had not fallen ere the enemy took to flight,
their bodies sword-scarred and punctured by lances.
The victors returned bearing aloft banners of glory.
And chanting songs of victory to the time of their
horses' hoofbeats, which fell upon the stones of the
valley like hammer blows.

They looked down upon the ravine, and the moon
rose from behind the mouth of the river. The mighty
towering rocks, rising with the spirits of the people,
appeared, and the forest of the cedars revealed itself
as though it were a sign of honor that past ages
had hung upon the breast of Lebanon.

They continued on their way, and the moonlight
shone on their weapons, and the distant caves
echoed their hymns, until they came to the foot of
an ascent, when they were halted by the neighing
of a horse. The beast stood among the gray-colored
rocks as though it were cut from them. The men
approached it, seeking the cause of the neighing,

and they stumbled across a dead body stubbed out on the ground whose blood mingled with the earth. Then the chief of the group shouted: "Show me the man's sword; I know its owner."

Some of the horsemen dismounted and surrounded the corpse. After a while one of them lifted his head and, looking toward the chief, said in a hoarse voice: "His fingers grasp the hilt of the sword tightly: it would be wrong to loose them."

Said another: "The weapon is sheathed with blood, and its metal cannot be seen."

A third one said: "The blood has congealed on hand and hilt and bound the blade to the arm and made them one."

Thereupon the leader dismounted and went over to the slain man and said: "Raise his head and let the moonlight show to us his face." The men hastened to do his bidding and the dead warrior's face was revealed from behind the veil of death. Its features were strong and told of courage and boldness and endurance; the face of a warrior speaking without voice of his manhood. The face of one sorrowing and rejoicing. The face of one who faced the foe with valor and met death with a smile. The face of a hero of Lebanon who was present that day in battle and saw the vanguard of victory but lived not to sing songs of triumph with his comrades.

And when they took off his head-cloth and wiped the dust of battle from his pale face, the leader cried out in a voice of pain: " 'Tis the face of Al-Sa'abi's son. Ah, the pity of it!" And the men echoed that name, sighing. Then they became silent as though their hearts, drunk with the wine of victory, were become sobered in an instant and had seen in the loss of a hero a thing greater than the might and glory of victory.

There they stood like stone images before the awe of this scene, and their tongues were dried up and they held their peace. For so do the brave in spirit in the face of death. Weeping and lament are for women; and crying and wailing are of children. For men of the sword there is naught but to stand in silence and awe. The silence that holds in grip strong spirits as the eagle's talons grip the throat of its prey. That silence which rises above weeping and lament; which in its sublimeness renders misfortune more awesome and terrifying. A silence causing the mighty spirit to descend firm mountain heights to the depths of the valley. A silence presaging the coming of the storm. And when the storm comes not is yet greater and mightier than it.

They removed the garments of the slain youth to see whereon death had placed its hand. On his breast were sword wounds agape like mouths afoam, speaking in the stillness of that night of the ambitions of men. The leader dropped on his knees by the dead man and, looking closely at the body, saw that a kerchief embroidered with gold thread was

163

tied round the forearm. He pondered on this, for he knew the hand that had spun the silk and the fingers that had worked the thread. Then he hid it away among the garments and withdrew a little, covering his own drawn face with a trembling hand. That same hand which had severed a head from a body now trembled and wiped away a tear. For it had touched the edge of a kerchief that beloved fingers had wound round the arm of a boy gone to do battle bravely. Now he was fallen and would return to her borne on the shoulders of his comrades.

And while the chieftain's spirit hovered thus between the horrors of death and mysteries of love, one of his men spoke and said:

"Come you, let us dig for him a grave under yonder oak tree. Its roots will drink from his blood, and its branches will flourish through his remains. 'Twill grow in strength and become immortal and will be a sign telling these knolls of his bravery and valor."

And another said: "Nay; let us carry him to the forest of the cedars and bring him by the church. There will his bones rest guarded by the shadow of the Cross against the Last Day."

And said another: "Bring you him here when his blood has fed the earth. And leave his sword in his right hand. Then plant his lance by his side and slay his beast over his grave. And let his weapon stay as a solace to him in his solitude."

"Bury not a sword stained with enemy blood, nor slay a yearling that has faced death. Do not abandon in the wilderness a weapon accustomed to an active hand and a strong forearm. Rather carry all back to his kinsman as a goodly inheritance." So spoke one.

Yet another raised his voice. "Let us kneel by his side and pray the prayers of the Nazarene, that Heaven might pardon him and bless our victory."

"Nay, let us raise him upon our shoulders and make our shields and lances as a bier to him; and encircle this valley, singing songs of victory. Let him look upon the slain of our foes, and the lips of his wounds shall smile ere they are closed by the earth of the grave."

"Let us lift him onto his steed and support him with the skulls of the killed and gird him with his lance and bring him into the quarters a victor. He submitted not to death till he had taken heavy count of the enemies' souls."

"Come, let us away and bid him farewell at the foot of this mountain. The echo from the caves shall be his companion and the ripple of the streams his comforter. His bones shall rest in the wilderness and hear the gentle tread of night's approach."

"Leave him not here, for in this place do dwell desolation and solitude. Rather do you carry him to the village burial place. There will he have the spirits of our fathers as comrades to speak with him in

165

the still night and recount to him their battle stories and tales of glory."

In that wise did they all speak.

Then their chief rose among them and made a sign for their silence. He drew a sigh and said:

"Trouble him not with memories of war; neither let the ears of his soul in flight listen more to tales of lances and swords. Suffer us to bear him in peace and quiet back to his birthplace. For there one sits watching for his homecoming. The spirit of a maiden waits upon his return from the slaughter. Let us, then, take him back to her that she be not denied the sight of his face and the kissing of his brow."

So they lifted him to their shoulders and bore him away, their heads and their eyes downcast. Behind them walked his sorrowing horse, its halter trailing on the ground. From time to time it neighed, and it was answered by the caves in echo. It was as if those caves had hearts and could feel with the heart in the extremity of its grief.

And so down that valley bathed in moonlight went the Procession of Victory behind the Cortege of Death. The Ghost of Love led them, dragging along his broken wings.

THE BEAUTY OF DEATH

Dedicated to M. E. H.

Let me sleep, for my soul is drunk of love;
Let me slumber, for my spirit is replete with the
    days and the nights.
Kindle the lights
And put fire to the censers about my couch;
Scatter around my body
Petals of the rose and narcissus,
And on my hair put pounded musk;
Pour out upon my feet
Goodly smelling perfumes.
Then behold, and read what is writ by death's hand
    upon my brow.

Leave me deep in the arms of slumber;
For mine eyelids are tired, and heavy with this
    wakefulness.
  Strike upon the lyre and the lute
And let the echo of their silvered strings
Fall and sway upon mine ears.
Blow upon the pipe and flute

And weave from their limpid notes
A veil about my heart,
The heart that hastens to its end.
Sing to me songs of Ruha
And from their enchanting cadence
Spread wide a carpet for my spirit,
Then look, and in my eyes
Will you behold the light of hope.

Dry then your tears, my friends,
Raise aloft your heads
As flowers lift up their crowns at dawn's breaking,
And behold Death's bride standing as a pillar of
    light
Between my bed and the void.
Still your breath awhile and hearken with me
To the fluttering of her wings.

* * *

Come you, children of my mother, say me farewell;
Kiss my brow with smiling lips,
Embrace my lips with your eyes
And kiss my eyelids with your lips.
Bring nigh the children to my bed,
Suffer them to caress my head
With fingers soft as the petal of a rose.
Bring near the aged to bless my brow
With fingers gnarled and withered.
Let the daughters of the quarter come

And see God's image in my eyes,
And hearken to the echo of an everlasting melody
    hastening with my spirit.

PARTING

Now I am come to the mountaintop,
And my spirit soars in the upper regions of freedom
    and release.
I am become far, far away, sons of my mother,
And the hill's face is hidden from mine eyes beyond
    the mist.
The emptiness of the valley is submerged in a sea
    of silence,
And the ways and passes erased by fingers of forget-
    fulness.
The meadows and the forest are concealed behind
    phantoms, white like clouds in spring,
And yellow as the sun's rays,
Red as the cloak of evening.

The song of the sea waves is stilled,
The music of the brooks in the fields grows faint,
And voices rising from the multitude are silenced.
I hear not any more save the hymn of Eternity,
Merging with the soul's desire.

REST

Unwrap my body of its linen shroud
And clothe me in leaves of lily and jasmine.
Take my remains out of this ivory casket
And lay them on a couch of orange blossom.
Lament not over me, sons of my mother,
But sing you songs of youth and joy.
Shed not tears, O daughter of the fields,
But chant a poem of days of the harvest and the
    pressing.
Cover not my breast with weeping and sighing,
But write upon it with your fingers
The symbol of love and the sign of joy.
Disturb not the air's repose
With the chanting of priest and threnody,
But let your heart to exult with me
In praise of immortality and everlasting life.

Wear not the black of mourning,
But rejoice with me in white raiment.
Speak not in sorrow of my going,
But close your eyes and you shall see me among
    you,
Now and forevermore.
Lay me down upon leafy boughs,
Raise me high upon shoulders,
Then lead me slowly to the wild places.

Carry me not to a burying-place,
For the multitude's clamor disturbs my rest,
And the rattling of bones and skulls robs me of
    slumber.
Bear me to the forest of cypress trees
And on that place where the violet and anemone
    grow
Dig me a grave.
Dig my grave deep,
That the floods bear not my bones to the valley.
Dig my grave wide,
That the phantoms of night may come and sit be-
    side me.

Cast aside these garments
And lead me naked to the earth's heart;
Lay me down softly
On my mother's breast.
Cover me with soft earth,
And with each sod
Sow the seeds of the wild rose and jasmine
That they may blossom upon my grave,
Nourished by the body's elements,
To grow and spread abroad
The fragrance of my heart;
And stand forth
Holding aloft in the sun's face
The secrets of my rest,
Swaying in the breeze

To tell the passer-by
Of my yearnings and my dreams that are gone.

Leave me now, sons of my mother —
Leave me in my aloneness.
Go hence with silent steps,
The going of the stillness in the empty valley.
Leave me in my solitude — and disperse
Like the almond and the apple blossom
Scattered by Nisan's * breath.
Return you to your dwelling-places
And there shall you find that which Death cannot
　　take
From you and me.
Leave now this place,
Whom you seek is gone far from this world.

* April's.

SONGS

A SONG

In the depths of my spirit is a song no words shall
    clothe;
A song living in a grain of my heart that will flow
    not as ink on paper.
It encompasses my feeling with a gossamer cloak,
And will not run as moisture on my tongue.
How shall I send it forth even as a sigh
Whilst I fear for it from the very air?
To whom shall I sing it that knows no dwelling
Save in my spirit?
I fear for it from the harshness of ears.

Did you look into my eyes, you had seen the image
    of its image;
Did you touch my fingertips, you had felt its trem-
    bling.

The works of my hand reveal it
Even as the lake mirrors the shining stars.

My tears disclose it
Even as dewdrops that proclaim the rose's secret as
    the warmth scatters them.

A song sent forth of silence,
Engulfed by clamor
And intoned by dreams.
A song concealed by awakening.

O people, 'tis the song of Love;
What Ishak * shall recite it?
Nay, what David shall sing it?

Its fragrance is sweeter than the jasmine's;
What throat shall enslave it?
More precious is it than the virgin's secret;
What stringed instrument shall tell it?
Who shall unite the sea's mighty roar
With the nightingale's trilling?
And the sigh of a child with the howling tempest?
What human shall sing the song of the gods?

* Ishak al-Mausili, celebrated Arabian musician (A.D. 767–
850).

SONG OF THE WAVE

I and the shore are lovers:
The wind unites us and separates us.

I come from beyond the twilight
to merge the silver of my foam with the gold of its
    sand;
And I cool its burning heart with my moisture.

At dawn's coming I read passion's law to my be-
    loved,
And he draws me to his breast.
At even I chant the prayer of longing,
And he embraces me.

I am fretful and without rest,
But my loved one is the friend of patience.
Comes the ebb and I embrace my love;
It flows, and I am fallen at his feet.

How I danced around the daughters of the sea
When they rose up from the depths
To sit upon the rocks
And behold the stars!
How I hearkened to the lover
Protesting his passion to a comely maid:
I did help him with sighing and moaning.
How I consorted with the rocks when they were
cold and still,
And caressed them, laughing, when they smiled
not!
How I delivered bodies from the deep
And brought them to the living!
In what measure did I steal from the depths
Pearls, and gave to the daughters of beauty!

* * *

In the still night when all created things embrace
the phantom of sleep, I alone am awake, now
singing, now sighing.
Alas, wakefulness has destroyed me, but I am a
lover and the truth of Love is awakening.

Behold my life;
As I have lived, so shall I die.

SONG OF THE RAIN

I am the silver threads
The gods cast down from the heights,
And Nature takes me to adorn the valleys.

I am the precious pearls
Scattered from Astarte's crown,
And the daughter of morning stole me to beautify
    the fields.

I weep and the hillocks smile;
I am abased and the flowers are lifted.

The cloud and the field are two lovers
And I a messenger bringing one to the other;
Slaking with abundance this one's thirst
And healing that one's sickness.

The voice of thunder and lightning's blades
Herald my coming;

The rainbow proclaims my journey's end.
So is earthly life,
Entering between the feet of wrath,
Departing between the peaceful hands of Death.

I rise from the lake's heart
And glide upon wings of air
Until I am a verdant garden.
Thereon I descend
And kiss the lips of its flowers
And embrace its boughs.

In the stillness, with my gentle fingers,
I tap upon window panes:
The sound thereof is a song known to feeling spirits.

I am created of the earth's heat
And I am its slayer —
So is the woman who prevails over a man by the
    force that she takes from him.

I am the sigh of the ocean
And heaven's tear,
And the smile of the field.
So is love —
A sign from the ocean of feeling;
A tear from the heaven of thought;
A smile from the field of the spirit.

SONG OF BEAUTY

I am the guide of love,
I am wine of the spirit,
I am food to the heart.

I am a rose;
I open my heart at daybreak; a maiden plucks me
    and kisses me and puts me to her breast.
I am the abode of happiness
And the source of joy.
I am the beginning of repose.

I am a gentle smile on the lips of a maid;
Youth beholds me, his toil is forgotten, and his life
    becomes a stage for sweet dreams.

I am the poet's imagination
And the artist's guide.
I am teacher to the music-maker.

I am the glance in the eye of a child
Beheld by a tender mother.
Before it does she pray and glorify God.

I appeared to Adam in Eve's image
And enslaved him.
I was revealed to Solomon in his beloved, and made
      him poet and sage.
I smiled on Helen,
And Troy was destroyed;
I crowned Cleopatra, and peace conquered the Nile.

I am as Destiny;
In this day I build,
On the morrow destroy.
I am God,
I quicken and make dead.

I am lighter than a sigh from the violet flower,
And mightier than the tempest.
I am a Truth, O people, yea, a Truth.

SONG OF HAPPINESS

Man is my beloved and I am his. I yearn toward him and he has longing for me.

Woe is me, for in his loving is a sharer who troubles me and torments him. She is a cruel mistress called Matter. Wheresoever we go does she follow like a guardian to rive us apart.

I seek my beloved in the wild places beneath the trees and beside the pools, and I find him not. For Matter has seduced him and is gone with him to the city, wherein are the multitude and corruption and wretchedness.

I seek him in the seats of learning and the temples of wisdom. But I find him not, for Matter, who wears a garment of earth, has led him thither to the walled places of selfulness where dwell those busied in paltry things.

I seek him in the field of contentment, but find him not, for mine enemy has bound him in the caverns of coveting and greed.

I called to him at the hour of dawn, and he hears me not, for his eyes are heavy with the sleep of avarice.

I caress him at the fall of even, when silence is sovereign and the flowers are aslumber. But he heeds me not, for his love of things of the morrow has taken him.

My beloved loves me. He seeks me in his deeds, but he shall not find me save in the actions of God.

He seeks my union in a palace of glory builded on the skulls of the weakly, and among silver and gold.

I shall not be sufficient unto him save in the house of simplicity, which the gods have builded on the banks of the stream of love.

He would embrace me before slayers and oppressors, yet I shall not let him to kiss my mouth except in solitude among the flowers of innocence.

He would that trickery be a mean between him and me; but I seek no mediator save a deed free from evil.

My beloved has learned clamor and tumult from mine adversary, Matter. I will teach him to shed tears of beseeching from the eyes of his spirit and sigh a sigh of contentment.

My beloved is mine and I am his.

SONG OF THE FLOWER

I am a word uttered by Nature,
Then taken back
And hidden in her heart,
And a second time uttered.
I am a star fallen from the blue sky
Upon a green carpet.

I am a daughter of the elements:
Carried in Winter,
Born of Spring,
Reared by Summer;
And Autumn lays me to rest.

I am a gift to lovers
And a nuptial crown.
I am the last offering of the quick to the dead.

With morning's coming
I and the breeze together

Proclaim the light.
At even the birds and I bid it farewell.

I sway upon the plains
And adorn them.
I breathe my fragrance to the air.
I embrace slumber,
And the manifold eyes of night look long upon me.
I seek awakening to look on the single eye of day.

I drink of the dew's intoxication
And hearken to the blackbird's song.
I dance to the rhythm of the grasses shouting;
I look ever heavenward to see the light,
Not to behold therein my image.
This is a wisdom man has not learned yet.

THE HYMN OF MAN

I was,
And I am.
So shall I be to the end of time,
For I am without end.

I have cleft the vast spaces of the infinite, and taken flight in the world of fantasy, and drawn nigh to the circle of light on high.

Yet behold me a captive of matter.

I have hearkened to the teachings of Confucius, and listened to the wisdom of Brahma, and sat beside the Buddha beneath the tree of knowledge.

Behold me now contending with ignorance and unbelieving.

I was upon Sinai when the Lord showed Himself to Moses. By the Jordan I beheld the Nazarene's miracles. In Medina I heard the words of the Apostle of Arabia.

Behold me now a prisoner of doubt.

I have seen Babylon's strength and Egypt's glory and the greatness of Greece. My eyes cease not upon the smallness and poverty of their works.

I have sat with the witch of Endor and the priests of Assyria and the prophets of Palestine, and I cease not to chant the truth.

I have learned the wisdom that descended on India, and gained mastery over poetry that welled from the Arabian's heart, and hearkened to the music of people from the West.

Yet am I blind and see not; my ears are stopped and I do not hear.

I have borne the harshness of unsatiable conquerors, and felt the oppression of tyrants and the bondage of the powerful.

Yet am I strong to do battle with the days.

All this have I heard and seen, and I am yet a child. In truth shall I hear and see the deeds of youth, and grow old and attain perfection and return to God.

I was,
And I am.
So shall I be to the end of time,
For I am without end.

A POET'S VOICE

Strength sows within the depths of my heart and I harvest and gather ears of corn and give it in sheaves to the hungry.

The spirit revives this small vine and I press its grapes and give the thirsty to drink.

Heaven fills this lamp with oil and I kindle it and place it by the window of my house for those that pass by night.

I do these things because I live by them, and were the days to forbid me and the nights stay my hand, I would seek death; for death is more meet to a prophet cast out by his nation and a poet who is an exile in his own land.

Mankind is disturbed as the tempest, and I sigh in silence. For I have found that the anger of the storm abates and is swallowed by the gulf of time; but a sigh endures with God's enduring.

Mankind clings to matter cold as snow. I seek love's flame to clasp to my breast that it may consume my vitals and make weak my bowels. For I have found that matter slays a man without pain, and love resurrects him in agony.

Mankind is divided into sects and tribes, and belongs to countries and territories.

I see myself a stranger in one land, and an alien among one people. Yet all the earth is my homeland, and the human family is my tribe. For I have seen that man is weak and divided upon himself. And the earth is narrow and in its folly cuts itself into kingdoms and principalities.

Humankind is gathered upon the destruction of the shrine of the spirit and helps build up temples of the body.

I stand alone in mourning, listening. And I hear from within me a voice of hope, saying:

"As love gives life to the human heart in travail, so does folly teach it the ways of wisdom. Pain and folly lead to a great joy and a perfect knowledge, for the Eternal Wisdom has created no thing in vain under the sun."

2

I stand alone in mourning, listening. And I hear those that dwell thereon for their weariness.

But did my people take up the sword, saying it was out of love of their land, and fall upon my neighbor's land and plunder its goods and slay its men and render its children orphans and make its women widows, and water its soil with its sons' blood and feed to the prowling beast the flesh of its youth, I would hate my land and its people.

I am kindled when I remember the place of my birth, and I lean in longing toward the house wherein I grew;

But should a wayfarer seek food and shelter in that house and its inhabitants turn him away, then would my joy be turned to mourning and my longing become a consoling, and I would say:

"In truth, the house that refuses bread to the needy and a bed to the seeker is most meriting of destruction and ruin."

I love the place of my birth with some of the love for my land;

I love my country with a little of my love for the world, my homeland;

I love the world with my all, for it is the pastureland of Man, the spirit of divinity on earth.

Sacred humanity is the spirit of divinity on earth. That humanity which stands amidst ruins clothing her nakedness in ragged garments, and shedding abundant tears upon her withered cheeks; calling upon her sons in a voice that fills the air with lament and mourning.

The sons that hear her not for the chanting of their battle hymns; who flee from her tears in the flashing of gleaming swords.

Humanity, who sits in her aloneness crying out to the people for succor and is not heeded. But did one among them draw near and dry her tears and comfort her in her affliction, then the others would say: "Forsake her, for tears make only the weak to grieve."

Humanity is the spirit of divineness on earth. Divineness walks among the nations speaking of love and pointing to the way of life.

And the multitude laughs and jeers at its words and teachings, which yesterday the Nazarene heard and for which He was crucified. Socrates, too, heard, and they gave him poison to drink.

Those today among the people who hear and say with the Nazarene and Socrates, them the multitude cannot kill, but they mock them, saying: "Scorn is harsher than death and more bitter."

Jerusalem was not able of the Nazarene's killing, for He lives eternally. Athens could not destroy Socrates, for he likewise lives.

Mockery and scorning shall not prevail against those that hearken to humanity and follow in the steps of the gods. They shall live forevermore.

3

You are my brother and we are the children of one universal holy spirit.

You are my likeness, for we are prisoners of two bodies formed of one clay.

You are my companion on the road of life and my helper in the understanding of a truth concealed beyond the clouds. You are man, but I have loved you, my brother.

Say of me what you will and the morrow will judge you, and your words shall be a witness before its judging and a testimony before its justice.

Take from me what you will, but you shall not plunder save the portion to which you have title and those things I took in my greed. You are worthy of a sum thereof, if that sum satisfy you.

Do with me what you will, for you are not able to touch my reality.

Spill my blood and pierce my body, but you shall not do hurt to my soul, neither shall you destroy it. Bind my hands and feet with bonds and cast me into the blackness of a prison cell. Yet you shall not prison my thought, for it is free as the breeze that passes through timeless and boundless space.

You are my brother and I love you.

I love you when you prostrate yourself in your mosque, and kneel in your church, and pray in your synagogue.

You and I are sons of one faith — the Spirit. And those who are set up as heads over its many branches are as fingers on the hand of a divinity that points to the Spirit's perfection.

I love you for the love of your truth arising from the minds of all people. That truth I see not now because of my blindness, but I hold it sacred because it is of the things of the Spirit. The truth that shall meet with my truth in the hereafter and merge the one with the other like the fragrance of flowers, and become one all-embracing and immortal with the immortality of Love and Beauty.

I love you, for I have seen you weak before the strong and the cruel; and poor and needy before the palaces of the endowed and the coveting.

So did I weep for your sake, and through my tears did I behold you in the arms of a justice that smiled on you and mocked at your tormentors.

You are my brother and I love you.

4

You are my brother. Why then do you contend with me?

Why come you to my land striving to humble me to satisfy them that would seek glory from your words and joy from your laboring?

Why do you forsake your wife and your young to pursue death to a far-off land for the sake of those that lead who would buy honor with your blood and high station with your mother's grief? Is it a noble thing that a man contend in battle with his brother?

Let us raise, then, an image to Cain and sing the praise of Hanan.

They do say, my brother, that the preserving of self is the first canon of nature. But I have seen those that covet privilege commend to you the abasement of self, the easier to enslave your brothers.

Likewise do they say that the love of existence makes incumbent the robbing of others of their right.

But I say that the protection of another's right is of the noblest and finest of men's acts.

And if my existence be the condition of another's destruction, then, say I, death were sweeter to me.

And if I found no honorable and loving person to kill me, then gladly by my own hand would I bear myself to eternity before its time.

Love of self, my brother, creates blind dispute, and disputing begets strife, and strife brings forth authority and power, and these are the cause of struggle and oppression.

The spirit deems the power of wisdom and justice above ignorance and tyranny. But it rejects that power which forges out of metal keen-edged swords to spread abroad ignorance and injustice.

That is the power which destroyed Babylon and razed Jerusalem to its foundations and brought low Rome;

The same that set up shedders of blood and slayers to whom the multitudes ascribed greatness;

whose names writers glorified; whose battles books rejected not to mention, as the earth failed not to carry them on its back when they dyed its face with innocent blood.

What, my brother, made you enamored of him that would deceive you, and made you crave him who did you hurt?

True power is a wisdom keeping guard over a just and natural law.

Where is the justice of sovereignty when it slays the slayer and imprisons the robber and then falls upon its neighbor and kills and plunders in its thousands?

What say the zealots of killers who punish murderers, and robbers who requite the plunderer?

You are my brother and I love you, and love is justice in its highest manifestation.

And if I be not just in my love for you in all lands, then I am naught save a deceiver concealing the evil of selfulness beneath love's fine raiment.

CONCLUSION

My spirit is to me a companion who comforts me when the days grow heavy upon me; who consoles me when the afflictions of life multiply.

Who is not a companion to his spirit is an enemy to people. And he who sees not in his self a friend dies despairing. For life springs from within a man and comes not from without him.

I came to say a word and I shall utter it. Should death take me ere I give voice, the morrow shall utter it. For the morrow leaves not a secret hidden in the book of the Infinite.

I came to live in the splendor of Love and the light of Beauty.

Behold me, then, in life; people cannot separate me from my life.

Should they put out my eyes I would listen to the songs of love and the melodies of beauty and gladness. Were they to stop my ears I would find joy in the caress of the breeze compounded of beauty's fragrance and the sweet breaths of lovers.

And if I am denied the air I will live with my spirit; for the spirit is the daughter of love and beauty.

I came to be for all and in all. That which alone I do today shall be proclaimed before the people in days to come.

And what I now say with one tongue, tomorrow will say with many.

A NOTE ON THE TYPE USED

This book has been set in a modern Linotype adaptation of a type designed by William Caslon, the first (1692–1766), greatest of English letter founders. The Caslon face, an artistic, easily read type, has had two centuries of ever increasing popularity in our own country — it is of interest to note that the first copies of the Declaration of Independence and the first paper currency distributed to the citizens of the new-born nation were printed in this type face.